Alaska on Foot

Alaska

Wilderness

Techniques

for the

Far North

Erik Molvar

on Foot

Photographs by the author

Illustrations by Elayne Sears

The Countryman Press

Woodstock, Vermont

The Countryman Press
PO Box 175
Woodstock, Vermont 05091–0175

Distributed by W.W. Norton & Company, Inc.
500 Fifth Avenue
New York, New York 10110

Library of Congress Cataloging-in-Publication Data
Molvar, Erik.
Alaska on foot : wilderness techniques for the Far North / Erik Molvar ;
photographs by the author.
          p.   cm.
Includes bibliographical references and index.
ISBN 0-88150-351-7 (alk. paper)
1. Backpacking—Alaska. 2. Wilderness survival—Alaska. 3. Camping—
Alaska—Safety measures. I. Title.
GV199.42.A4M65   1996
796.5'1'09798—dc20
95-39146
CIP

Maps by XNR Productions, © 1996 The Countryman Press
Text design by Kit Kuntze
Cover photo by Erik Molvar
Cover design by Triebert Ross Design

 **PRINTED IN CANADA**
10 9 8 7 6 5 4 3 2 1

For

ABBIE JOHNSON *&* MELANIE WIKE

my favorite Alaskan hiking partners

Acknowledgments

The techniques presented here have been shared with me by fellow backpackers and by teachers over the course of many years. It would be impossible to credit all of those people here, but I would like to thank Bill Brockman for introducing me to backpacking and for encouraging my appreciation for wilderness those many years ago. Bob Piorkowski gave this book its first real critique and added to it his wisdom from decades of living in the Alaskan bush. Sandy Kogl, David N. Cole, David Klein, Jon Nierenburg, Wayne Merry and Debbie Miller also provided valuable input. Thanks to the editing staff at The Countryman Press for polishing my rough-hewn prose.

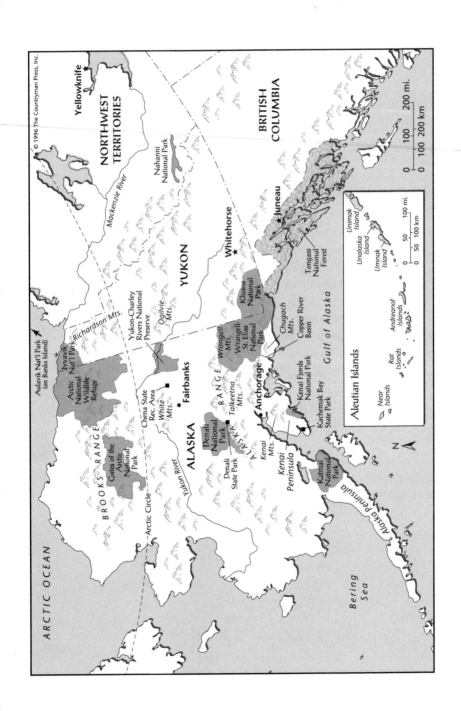

Contents

Introduction

ALASKA is the last bastion of wilderness in the United States. It is a land of extremes: long summer days, frigid winters when the sun disappears for months, bustling cities, mind-boggling distances uninterrupted by human intrusions. It is an unforgiving country, and even experienced outdoor folk are occasionally swallowed up by the vastness of the landscape as their reward for taking chances and pushing personal limits. In many cases, backpacking routines that are the accepted norm in the lower 48 states do not apply to Alaska. In addition, the explorer who visits the Far North will frequently be confronted by obstacles and dangers that are completely foreign. For example, few backpackers ever have the need to master river crossings, choose routes across an untracked landscape, or negotiate glaciers. This book presents the additional know-how to help hikers and backpackers adjust their techniques to meet the challenges of the Arctic and subarctic wilderness. The techniques discussed within, though tailored specifically to Alaska, apply equally to the Yukon and Northwest Territories of neighboring Canada.

Alaska represents the last region of this country where whole ecosystems function much as they did before the coming of humans. The Alaska Natives traditionally saw themselves as part of the greater whole of nature, and built their culture around the natural rhythms of the Alaskan wilderness. As a result, they left little evidence of their passage, and the land thrived under their stewardship. The fact that this magnificent land exists in its present pristine state owes a large debt to the harmonious folkways of these original Alaskans. We have inherited the challenge to keep it wild and pristine in the face of increasing human use. One has only to look southward for a reminder of the misuse and overexploitation that the seemingly inexhaustible expanse of the Alaskan wilderness would suffer. As wilderness travelers, it is incumbent upon each of us to tread lightly on the landscape, and, like the Inuit, Salish, and Athapaskans before us, to leave no trace of our passage.

The Making of the Great Land

Alaska is still a landscape in the making. Colliding land masses push the cloud-scraping spires of the Alaska Range higher each year. Enormous glaciers gouge deep valleys in the mountains, and whittle the peaks into sharp horns and the ridges into knife-edged arêtes. From the peaks, young rivers course down braided channels to the lowlands, moving tons of alluvial gravel each year. Along the coast, active volcanoes belch fire and ash into the sky, and send down rivers of molten lava to create anew a desolate volcanic moonscape. This youthful and ever-changing landscape is bathed in summer by the midnight sun, and showered in winter by the silent curtains of the aurora borealis. It is the same vast wilderness that always was, and—with the help of our good judgment and protection—always will be.

At the close of the Pleistocene Epoch some 10,000 years ago, enormous ice sheets covered much of North America. Much of the planet's water was locked up in glacial ice, lowering ocean levels and exposing a broad isthmus that connected present-day Alaska with Siberia. A diverse assemblage of ice-age mammals dispersed across this Bering land bridge, bound for the ice-free steppes that covered interior Alaska and parts of the Yukon. Many members of Alaska's Pleistocene fauna have gone extinct: The woolly mammoth, steppe bison, cave lion, dire wolf, short-faced bear, and giant ground sloth are found no more on the Alaskan tundra. Some Asian species, such as saiga antelope, primitive horses, and camels, flourished here during the Pleistocene but ultimately disappeared from the Western Hemisphere. Enormous ancestors of the moose, caribou, bi-

Perhaps the hallmark landscape of Alaska is the open tundra.

son, beaver, and Dall sheep that still inhabit the state once shared the steppes with these exotic mammals.

Small bands of neolithic hunter-gatherers soon followed this influx of animals into North America, and dispersed throughout this ice-free wilderness. They found a steppe grassland rich in game, and though the hunters were never populous, their stone microblades have been found throughout the North Country. Polar seas were probably covered by a permanent ice cap at this time, and as a result the Arctic air masses that swept across ancient Alaska carried little moisture. Colder temperatures prevented melting, however. Long valley glaciers extended out onto the lowlands from the Alaska and Brooks Ranges, and the Chugach and Wrangell Mountains were completely mantled in icefields during the height of the ice ages.

Since the Pleistocene, white spruce forests have moved up from the south, spreading throughout the interior of Alaska. Willows have also expanded their range northward, and continue to do so in historical times. Along with these expanding plant communities has come the influx of animals associated with these habitats, most notably moose. In some respects, the landscape offers glimpses into the ice-age past of our continent. There are many ranges that still harbor vast icefields, where isolated island peaks, called nunataks, are the only visible rock. Extensive valley glaciers pour downward from these ice sheets and, when they retreat, expose virgin soil to colonizing plants. Strong winds send great clouds of glacial dust aloft from the toes of the retreating glaciers and deposit their loads many miles from the source. This is the same process by which the loess soils of the American heartland were formed. The newly bared earth at the foot of the glacier becomes colonized by a succession of pioneering plants, in the same pattern once seen across our continent following the end of the ice ages.

Perhaps the hallmark landscape of Alaska is the open tundra. It is found in a broad swath across the northern third of the state, and in vast pockets among the high mountains. Tundra ecosystems are dominated by a single factor: cold. Tundra is typically underlain by permafrost, a soil that is frozen throughout the year. Only the top layers of the soil thaw during the summer months, and cool soil temperatures hamper the growth of soil microbes, slowing decomposition to a snail's pace. Plants must complete all of their growth for the year in the 2- to 3-month period when the tundra is snow-free. Perennial flowers must sprout, flower, and set seed in this brief span of time. Woody plants flatten themselves against the ground so that their tender buds do not protrude above the insulating surface of the snow. There are several species of willow found here that never exceed several inches in height. Look closely at the uniform mat of the tundra and you will discover a hidden world of miniature plants and animals.

The primeval landscape of Alaska is home to the most diverse assemblage of wild animals in the Northern Hemisphere. The incursions of man are still relatively limited, and the Alaskan bush harbors complete ecosystems that still function much as they did before the arrival of Europeans. The grizzly bear occupies the top niche in the food chain, and the vast herds of caribou course through a landscape unfettered by roads and fences. The howl of the wolf can be heard in all corners of the state, and moose claim their share of ownership in the few small cities. Here, ecologists can study the unique processes that occur only in unfragmented ecosystems, and backcountry explorers can become a part of a natural flow of life unimpeded by the incursions of human civilization.

Even so, the Alaskan wilderness has seen the passage of humans for millennia. For the most part, the Inuit, Aleut, and Athapaskan peoples moved across the landscapes like ghosts, leaving few traces of their passage. Native settlements were typically located along rivers and coastlines, which served as the main travel corridors. In the 1700s, Russian fur traders built settlements along the coast, and introduced Eastern Orthodox Christianity to the natives that lived there. The United States bought the Russian territory of Alaska in 1867, and soon a trickle of Anglo prospectors infiltrated the most remote corners of the new territory. The gold rush passed quickly, but furs continued to provide a steady income for bush dwellers well into the 20th century. The cabins and well-built caches constructed along their traplines still stand today in isolated parts of the Alaskan bush. In the dry climate of interior Alaska and the Yukon, historical structures deteriorate slowly, and many are still standing today to remind us of our predecessors who struggled to make a better life in the northern wilds. These fascinating historical sites are not renewable. Enjoy them where you find them, and leave them undisturbed for the next traveler to discover.

Exploring Alaska on Foot

It is important to point out that although the Alaskan wilderness seems to present limitless options to the foot traveler, there comes a point where the terrain becomes too steep to tackle safely without specialized mountaineering skills and equipment. For the purposes of this book, lands with a slope greater than 45 degrees, as well as glaciers that have a substantial slope or are snow-covered, are considered technical terrain and beyond the scope of our discussion. There are some fine mountaineering books on the market, but such skills are almost impossible to master from printed text alone. This author recommends that anyone interested in venturing onto technical terrain undertake a well-respected climber's course in order to master the essential skills of this dangerous sport. Hikers, backpackers, hunters, and anglers will have little trouble finding a rewarding backcountry experience without venturing onto this vertical part of the landscape.

Backpacking has inherent dangers that the best knowledge and skill cannot completely eliminate. It is an exercise in self-reliance, and thus judgment and common sense must be applied at every turn. Explorers who familiarize themselves with the landscape, its pitfalls and hazards, and the techniques needed to overcome them can significantly reduce the odds of catastrophe. But the possibility of danger cannot be eliminated, even by the best-trained expert. We who take to the Alaskan wilds must accept these inherent dangers as part of the experience, and use preparation and good judgment to overcome the capricious wiles of the Arctic. It is our hope that this guide will help Arctic travelers achieve a backcountry experience that is as safe as it is rewarding.

By far the largest state in the union, Alaska has fewer residents than any other state except Wyoming. At the last census, there were still almost as many caribou as humans living here. The Alaskan wilderness is as pristine and untrammeled as any in the world, and offers limitless possibilities for exploration. Most of the popular backpacking destinations are completely free of trails, and visitors are expected to select their own routes and must navigate for themselves. Beginning backpackers should hone their skills in the relative safety of the lower 48 states before attempting a prolonged expedition into the trackless wilds of the North Country. Inexperienced travelers can get their feet wet with day trips, or with overnighters into places like the Kenai Mountains that have developed trail systems. There are a number of good introductory texts on backpacking, so this guide will not go into long-winded discussions on the fundamentals of the sport.

1 Planning Your Trip

IN terms of an expedition's success, solid preparation is as important as ability in determining the quality of your backcountry experience. These preparations should encompass every aspect of your trip, from choosing an area to explore to selecting the right equipment. Alaska offers a broad spectrum of wilderness experiences for hikers of all abilities and incomes. If you prepare well and do your homework on the area you will be exploring, you are almost guaranteed to have a great experience, regardless of the challenges that arise unexpectedly.

Before leaving home, gather as much information as you can that is pertinent to the local area you intend to explore. Guidebooks are a good place to start, but often contain information of a very general nature. The land management agencies that administer the territory you intend to cross are excellent sources of information; they often have descriptive pamphlets that are available free of charge. Addresses and phone numbers for land management agencies can be found in the "The Explorer's Directory" at the back of this book. Finally, topographic maps, which show the contours of the landscape, are indispensable for evaluating the practicality of different routes. Once you have assembled the necessary information, you will be able to formulate a mental image of the specific challenges that lie ahead.

Once you get to Alaska, try to identify local sources of information. In addition to information centers and ranger stations, local residents can be a wellspring of knowledge about terrain or conditions. Alaskans as a whole are friendly and helpful, but many are a bit leery of tourists. The best way to approach them is with an attitude of innocent humility: Engage them in friendly, social conversation aimed at finding out about local conditions. The pace of life is a little slower up here, and it's best not to rush your hosts. Let them spin their yarns at full length, and they will get to the point in their own good time.

Some of the information you might ask for changes throughout the year, so it cannot be packaged in a pamphlet. Ask about snow conditions on the high passes, and about the depths of streams and rivers that you plan to cross. Ask about bear sightings, and pay particular attention to stories of problem bears or sows with cubs. Ask about caribou calving grounds and other critical habitats that you should avoid while traveling. Ask what the prevailing vegetation is like, and whether there are any dense brushfields or impenetrable bogs along the way. Finally, describe your intended route to the locals, who might be able to tell you about unforeseen obstacles.

The Ideal Hiking Party

Many hikers have the immense good fortune to explore the backcountry with trusted friends who have shared numerous expeditions into the wilds. This ideal situation may not always occur, and you should be aware that minor friction between individuals can be magnified into major problems in the isolation of the backcountry. When assembling your hiking partners in preparation for a trip, bear in mind that each person will bring different abilities and expectations into the backcountry. Hash out your collective expectations beforehand, and make sure that you are prepared to deal with potential problems. Backcountry travel is known as roughing it for good reason—it offers a primitive (although healthy) experience devoid of modern conveniences. Cultivating a stoic attitude in the face of hardships will provide the cement that bonds your hiking party together and ensure that a good time is had by all.

This is especially important if you or other members of your party are new to backpacking; experienced group members should prepare newcomers by explicitly explaining the dangers and hardships that lie ahead and the level of performance that will be expected. When hiking with novices, it often helps to lighten their loads at the expense of experienced backpackers, who should have no problems with the added weight. Most new backpackers will be eager to prove their ability to cope with novel situations, and will perform well if properly prepared.

The composition of your group may contribute to the successes or shortfalls of your hiking trip. It is best if you have at least one experienced backpacker in your midst whose wisdom you can draw upon in unusual situations. At least one person should be well versed in wilderness first aid; ideally, each member of your party will have some basic first-aid training. It is also helpful to have each group member research one particular facet of your target landscape. Perhaps one group member could read up on local geology, a second on regional wildlife, while a third could tackle indigenous plants. This strategy will give each group member a greater feeling of indispensability and will enrich the experience of all members of the group.

The ideal group size for backpacking seems to be three or four. This number allows you to split up the heavy gear and lighten everyone's load. In case of sickness or injury, it also allows one person to go for help while another remains with the victim. However, smaller groups have a statistically greater probability of surprising grizzly bears during the course of their travels, and must take extra precautions to avoid doing so. Avoid traveling in groups of over 10 people, because it will be difficult to find campsites, and impacts on the landscape will be magnified by groups of this size. Large groups should split up into more manageable units, and camp some distance apart.

Because each hiker has different desires and expectations, planning the perfect trip becomes more complex as you increase the size of your group. Choose your hiking partners carefully, because you will be in close contact with each of them throughout your trip. Discord becomes increasingly likely with larger party sizes, and it may become difficult to keep the group together. Avoid conflicts by planning out details beforehand, including how many miles the party should cover each day, what routes will be taken, and so forth. Be certain that faster hikers are prepared to slow down to wait for slower members of the party, and that slow hikers are willing to make an honest effort to keep up. Remember that maintaining group harmony is at least as important as weather and terrain in determining the quality of a backcountry experience.

Solo backpacking in Alaska is certainly the ultimate test of self-reliance. For decades, park rangers have railed against soloing, citing the increased probability of lone backpackers getting into trouble and the difficulty of their getting out in the event of injury. Without a doubt, these risks are real: Statistics on grizzly bear encounters show that most maulings involve solo hikers, and there has never been a mauling that involved a group larger than five. It is a rather hard-and-fast rule that only expert backpackers should travel alone, and when doing so should take special care to avoid risky circumstances. I, for one, am much more cautious when I am alone in the backcountry, and am actually more likely to do something unwise in the security of a group. In the course of thousands of miles of solo backpacking in the most hostile and demanding environments in North America, I have yet to get into an emergency situation. Nonetheless, I know of this having happened to other solo travelers in Alaska, with deadly results. Hikers and backpackers who travel solo into the Alaskan wilds should recognize the complications that can arise in the event of sickness or injury, and must assume the responsibility for the added risks inherent in this activity.

Setting Your Sights

When selecting an area to explore, you should evaluate the landscape's potential to provide what you are looking for, as well as your own abilities and limitations in taking on the challenge of a backcountry expedition. If you push yourself too hard, you will be unable to appreciate fully even the most stunning landscapes because your mind will be focused on your own misery. You should plan your trip with an eye toward staying within your own limitations and those of your partners. Doing so will allow you ample time and energy to enjoy the wonderful Alaskan backcountry.

Cross-country travel, which is the rule rather than the exception in much of the Alaskan wilds, takes much more time than covering a similar distance on a trail. In general, a strong backpacker can rarely cover more than 2 miles an hour, even on an ideal hiking surface; challenging terrain may slow you down to a mere crawl. With this in mind, you should pace your trip so that you have sufficient time and energy to reach your destination each evening. Eight miles a day is a good maximum for seasoned hikers, while less experienced parties might set a slower pace.

Before you ever get to the trailhead, chart your course on your topographic map (see "Maps and Navigation"). Ask yourself, What possible barriers could block our intended path? Perhaps there are streams or rivers that might become swollen following a rainstorm. High passes may become snowbound in a freak storm. A sow grizzly and her cubs may decide to forage in the midst of your planned route. You should think about all of these possibilities before ever setting out, and make contingency plans in case you need to change your itinerary. Map out alternate routes of travel, including the fastest way back to civilization in the event that one of your party is injured. Finally, bring enough food and fuel for an extra couple of days in case an unforeseen occurrence extends your trip.

Weather or Not

Alaskan weather is as unpredictable as it is strange. In the mountains, drenching rain may soak travelers in one valley, while brilliant sunshine pours down upon backpackers just a couple of valleys away. According to Alaskan wisdom, "If you don't like the weather here, wait 5 minutes and it will change."

For this reason, you should never cancel a trip on account of rain, because the sun might be out in full force the following day. By the same token, clear skies are no guarantee of good weather, and you should always prepare for foul weather when loading your pack, even for brief day hikes. On average, you will probably experience some poor weather and some sunshine on any given trip. Prior weather events may force you to change your travel route or itinerary: Heavy snows may close passes, and rainstorms or glacial melting may flood rivers and make them impossible to cross. Check locally to get the latest information before you start off.

During the summer, Alaskan weather varies widely by region. The southeastern panhandle is characterized by cloudy and misty weather, with frequent rains. Sunshine is more common during the autumn, but the mountains may be invisible during much of the summer. This region experiences high temperatures ranging from 50 to 60 degrees Fahrenheit and cool evenings. The southern coast of mainland Alaska has similar weather, but sunshine prevails there about half the time. The Aleutians are known for their pea soup fogs, and sudden storms may blow up out of the Bering Sea at any time.

Chaotic weather characterizes the Alaska Range and other interior mountains, with brief clear spells interrupting rain and snow showers. Tall peaks like Denali create their own weather, and Denali itself is only visible about 30 percent of the time during the summer months. Daytime temperatures can reach the high 70s, while nights are too brief to become much cooler. However, periodic storms can bring snowy weather at any time during the year.

The lowlands of the interior typically experience cloudless days, and temperatures often soar into the high 90s. Rains are brief and uncommon, and tend to take the form of afternoon thundershowers. This weather pattern also prevails across most of the Yukon.

In the Brooks Range and on the North Slope, weather alternates between clear spells and rains that may last longer than a

Tundra vista, late evening in the Brooks Range

week. During the wet weather, the cloud deck often extends down to several hundred feet above sea level, thus obscuring the mountains. High temperatures range into the upper 60s, while cold snaps can bring the temperature down below the freezing point.

The shoulder seasons of spring and fall can provide some spectacular hiking experiences, but the weather is much riskier during these times. Spring hikers are likely to encounter deep snows throughout the state, and skis and snowshoes remain the preferred method of travel well into May in the colder regions. Melting snow raises creeks and rivers to flood levels, making crossings impossible in most cases. In fall, the clear days of summer give way to turbulent skies as waves of storms sweep the state, depositing blankets of snow in the high country and torrential rains in warmer areas. A brief Indian summer may put in appearances as late as October, but fall travelers should prepare for the worst and plot courses that avoid river fords.

Highlights of the Alaskan Calendar

The calendar of the Far North is punctuated by natural events that mark the changes of the seasons. Alaskans are proud of their four seasons: winter, June, July, and August. Each season has its own special charms and challenges, and you should plan your trip with these in mind. Depending on when you find yourself in Alaska, you may be able to enjoy some uniquely Alaskan activities and phenomena.

Spring may come to Alaska as early as mid-March, but snow persists on the ground until late May in most places. The major event during this time of year is spring breakup, when the icebound rivers of the interior break free of their frozen mantles. This event can occur from mid-April to early May. The ice cracks apart with explosive force, and floes are carried off downstream, perhaps to raft together in natural dams before breaking loose once more.

This is a period of transition in the Alaskan bush. The river ice that once served as highways for dogsleds and snow machines now forms impassable barriers to travel. As the snows melt, bush communities plan for the upcoming summer, when boats and airplanes become the primary methods of transport. It is also the season of cabin fever, when snowbound Alaskans increase their activity levels in response to the increased daylight but have a hard time traveling far afield.

Trees begin to leaf out long before the snow has left the ground, and smaller plants explode in a profusion of green as soon as the ground is warmed by the sun's rays. The first migratory birds arrive while the landscape is still seemingly in the grip of winter, and indeed, the Arctic winds may produce winterlike snowstorms well into June. As soon as the snow cover departs, wild animals become very active, feeding on the lush vegetation and giving birth to their young. Travel is difficult in springtime on account of the deep snow that still blankets shaded forests, and streams remain covered with thin layers of ice. It is a wonderful time for cross-country skiing and dogsledding, however, as the warm temperatures and good snow conditions make for ideal day trips and even overnight expeditions.

Rising temperatures and periodic rainstorms herald the coming of full summer in mid-June. Mosquitoes and other insect pests become abundant at this time and persist through the brief northern summer. Flowers abound, and the verdant landscape vibrates with life. Backcountry travel becomes easier as the summer progresses; in June, streams swollen with spring runoff are still difficult to cross and snowdrifts may yet cover high mountain passes. These conditions may prevail until mid-July in high-elevation areas. In the interior, fire danger is high during the long dry spells of summer, and thus special care must be taken to avoid starting a forest fire.

In mid-August, the leaves of tundra shrubs begin to turn red and gold with the first hints of autumn. Berries ripen, and animals forage intensively to prepare for the long winter months ahead. At the lower elevations, summer may linger on into September. Mosquitoes are generally killed off by the first hard frost, which may happen in early August at high elevations. However, the boreal forests of the Canadian northlands experience their heaviest hatches of blackflies at this time. With September comes the rutting season for moose and caribou, and the aspen and birch of the boreal forest turn all aflame with golden leaves. The first serious snowstorms hit the lower elevations in mid-September, although they may arrive earlier north of the Arctic Circle and at high elevations. By mid-October, the landscape is locked in snow, held fast in winter's unrelenting grip until the following spring.

Alaskan winters are long and cold. Short days and extreme temperatures force many folks to remain indoors for most of the winter, and inactivity and darkness combine to foster depression in many who overwinter here. Dogsledding, cross-country skiing, snowshoeing, and ski-jouring (which is accomplished by attaching a Nordic skier to a sled dog with a tow rope) are the most popular winter pastimes. Alaska receives few visitors during the winter, and the extreme dangers associated with winter expeditions preclude all but the most hardy souls from venturing into the backcountry at this time of year.

The Midnight Sun

The renowned midnight sun of Alaska has attained legendary status in the folklore of the North. Far from being a tall tale invented by half-mad prospectors, this phenomenon is the defining factor of daily rhythms in Alaska during the summertime. With the progression of spring into summer, the dark hours shrink with each passing day, until finally all that remains of the nighttime is a dusky gloom in the wee hours of the morning. Even at comparatively low latitudes, the sun may not set until 11 PM at the height of summer, bathing the landscape in wan light well into the night.

The Arctic Circle is defined as the place from which the sun never sets on the summer solstice, June 21, the longest day of the year. On this day, the sun rolls completely around the horizon, dipping in the north at midnight but never setting. The summer solstice is an important event in the Alaskan calendar, and many northern communities celebrate it with special festivities. The Arctic Circle, some 60 air miles north of Fairbanks at 66°33' north latitude, can be reached easily by automobile via the Dalton Highway. The unceasing rays of the solstice can also be viewed from Eagle Summit on the Steese Highway, by virtue of the high elevation of the White Mountains. North of the Arctic Circle, the sun may not pass below the horizon for weeks at a time. By the same token, the sun never rises on the winter solstice (December 21) north of the Arctic Circle, and in far northern villages like Barrow, night may reign continuously for several months.

The absence of night during the height of summer can play havoc with the sleep schedules of visitors. Indeed, during the summer's peak, the terms *night* and *day* have meaning only with regard to custom, and many Alaskans remain active well into the early hours of morning. It seems that the body requires less sleep during these long days, and many Alaskans get by on 4 or 5 hours of sleep a night and feel quite refreshed in the morning. Those who are accustomed to sleeping in darkness may have difficulty adjusting to the increased day length found at northern latitudes. Newcomers typically sleep very little during their first week or so in Alaska, and then become exhausted and regain their ability to sleep more regular hours.

The Northern Lights

The aurora borealis, or northern lights, is a celestial phenomenon that occurs year-round in far northern latitudes. (The Southern Hemisphere has its own counterpart, the aurora australis.) On clear nights, the shimmering auroral curtains move sinuously across the sky, changing form and color in a celestial dance of light. This natural light show enthralled American naturalist John Muir, who described the aurora as "this glory of light, so pure, so bright, so enthusiastic in motion." These silent symphonies of light have long been a symbol for the loneliness of the northern wilds; poet Robert Service immortalized the phenomenon in his ballad "The Shooting of Dan Mc-Grew":

* * *

Were you ever out in the Great Alone,
when the moon was awful clear,
And the icy mountains hemmed you in
with a silence you most could hear;
With only the howl of the timber wolf,
and you camped there in the cold,
A half-dead thing in a stark, dead world,
clean mad for the muck called gold;
While high overhead, green, yellow, and red,
The North Lights swept in bars?—
Then you've a hunch what that music meant. . .
hunger and night and the stars.

* * *

The aurora is formed by charged particles entering the atmosphere near the earth's magnetic poles. Storms on the surface of the sun, in the form of sunspots and solar flares, fling enormous quantities of charged atoms into space. This phenomenon is known as the solar wind. When the solar wind reaches earth, it is sucked into the atmosphere near the poles by the earth's magnetic field. As the charged particles cascade through the atmosphere, they form the luminous sheets of energy known as the aurora. The color of the aurora depends largely on the type of charged atom that is excited by the solar radiation. For the most part, the northern lights take on shades of white and pale green. On occasion, however, blue, reddish, purple, and pink auroras are seen.

The northern lights are visible only in a dark sky, and for this reason, visitors who arrive in Alaska in midsummer may miss them entirely due to round-the-clock daylight. The best times for viewing the lights seem to be spring and fall, although late August occasionally produces some spectacular shows. The aurora is typically most intense around midnight, and may persist until 3 or 4 in the morning. Auroras are occasionally seen to penetrate the clouds, creating a bizarre, brooding effect. Because solar storms are periodic in nature, the northern lights may be quite active for several days, and then disappear entirely for long periods of time.

Tourist Season

Each summer, a veritable flood of tourists engulfs the state of Alaska, clogging highways and crowding parks and museums. Many of these tourists come on package tours and are herded from site to site in a madcap effort to see "everything" in a span of a few days. Others sail the oceangoing ferryliners of the Inside Passage to Alaska, or drive the Alaska Highway comfortably behind the wheels of enormous campers replete with all the comforts of home. Many of these visitors seek the "Alaskan experience," featuring miles of trackless wilderness and utter solitude. Fortunately, this experience is available even at the height of tourist season (late June through July), but you must look beyond the strip malls and visitor centers in order to find it.

At parks and historic sites, most visitors are funneled into interpretive centers and roadside nature walks. This is a boon to vacationers, who can then learn about the environment without having to undertake long trips, and can use their time quite efficiently to get the most out of their park experience. At the same time, this policy benefits solitude-seeking hikers, because most visitors never get more than a mile from the road system. This leaves the entire span of the backcountry open for exploration, and makes solitude easy to find for those willing to take a hike.

Nevertheless, travelers who seek solitude are well advised to avoid the most popular times and places. Most Alaskans are heavily outdoor-oriented, so that weekends and holidays herald a substantial influx of people into backcountry areas. Some areas, most notably Denali National Park, have quota systems in which a limited number of permits are issued for various regions. These permits are typically hard to come by for the most popular areas during the peak season of use. Campgrounds and motels fill up well in advance for most hot-ticket parks, and reservations are recommended. Because of the limited supply of motel rooms in Alaska, rates may double and even triple during the height of the tourist season. Visitors who travel in the off-seasons will encounter much better rates, and will have a greater chance of finding solitude at their destination of choice. (However, many merchants reduce or discontinue their services during the off-seasons.) Backpackers can further their chances for solitude by avoiding lakes and streams that are fishing destinations, and by planning their trips into the many parts of Alaska that are less well known. Chapter 2 contains descriptions of hiking areas both popular and remote for travelers who seek all levels of wilderness experience.

Wildflowers

Because of the short growing season, flowers are in evidence from the thawing of the snowdrifts in spring and may continue to bloom beyond the first frost. Late June and early July typically produce the greatest diversity and abundance of plants in bloom. Most plants are biennial or perennial in these high latitudes, meaning that they live through at least one winter before flowering. Plants that store nutrients from the previous summer tend to flower early in spring, while plants that flower each year often flower in mid- to late summer.

You can find the widest variety of flowering plants in bloom by looking at a broad spectrum of elevations in the same general area; lower elevations will contain late-blooming plants, while early-blooming plants can be found in flower at the same time farther up the slope. In general, alpine areas are inhabited by plants that are typically found in the lowlands farther north. In addition, the severe cold winds and short growing seasons found at higher elevations often produce dwarf versions, as is the case with the alpine forget-me-not, which is much smaller than its low-elevation cousin.

Hunting Season

Alaska offers some of the finest hunting opportunities anywhere. Sportsmen come from all over the world to hunt here, and the employment of hunting guides contributes substantially to the Alaskan economy. Nowhere else in this country is hunting so integrated into the culture of a single state. The Alaska Department of Fish and Game has a complicated set of regulations that ensures that populations of game animals remain at healthy levels. The state is divided into a series of game management units, each of which may have different seasons and bag limits. Local residents, many of whom hunt during the regular sport season, may participate in special subsistence hunts at other times of the year. In fact, subsistence hunting by Alaska Natives and local residents provides an important source of food. Nonresidents who hunt in Alaska must be accompanied by an Alaskan resident or a licensed guide, and must pay rather expensive fees for a license and tags.

Hikers and backpackers who venture into the Alaskan wilds should be aware of hunting seasons in the local area and plan their trips accordingly. Sport hunting is generally allowed on all public lands with the exception of national parks and heavily populated areas. Some national parks have extensions called national preserves, and hunting is allowed there, too. Predictably, the heaviest hunting pressure is close to the roads, but guides and outfitters use charter planes to take groups of clients deep into the heart of the Alaskan wilderness.

If you are backpacking into an area during hunting season, wear bright clothing (blaze orange is best). Try to stay as visible as possible and avoid prowling about in dense brush. Most hunters are quite responsible, but it only takes one careless nimrod to put an end to your hiking career.

In general, the big-game hunting season opens in late August with hunts for Dall sheep. These animals are confined to the high mountains, so hikers who are traveling at lower elevations during this time period do not have to worry about hunters. Caribou and moose hunting begin from early to late September, depending on the local area. This coincides with the rut for both of these animals. Black and grizzly bears can be hunted at roughly the same time. The big-game season ends in mid-November, although some areas have a spring hunt for black bears. Copies of hunting regulations and season schedules can be obtained free of charge at local stores, or can be ordered by mail from the Alaska Department of Fish and Game.

Salmon Runs

The timing of salmon and steelhead runs varies from river to river, and different species may run in the same river at different times. A complete listing of major salmon runs can be found in "The Explorer's Directory" at the back of this book. In general, salmon runs peak in mid- to late summer, and create a fishing bonanza unparalleled in all the world. Anglers stand elbow to elbow along popular stream courses, competing for salmon in a mad frenzy known as "combat fishing." Anglers seeking peace and solitude should be prepared to walk for several miles from the nearest road; thankfully, most salmon fishermen never make it beyond sight of their vehicles.

Berry Season

In mid- to late August as summer is turning to autumn, a variety of bushes develop edible berries that provide a boon for hikers and bears alike. Berries tend to ripen earliest at the lower elevations, and southern regions produce berries earlier than northern ones. The initial flush of ripening produces the most overwhelming quantities of fruit; later in the year the availability of berries is less reliable. The berries that survive the feeding frenzy of humans, birds, and bears remain on the stem into the fall, and are often still palatable after they are frozen. Indeed, berries are an important winter food source for many birds that overwinter in Alaska. Edible berries are discussed in detail in Chapter 9.

2 Where to Go

ALASKA is an immense state with a broad spectrum of landscapes and hiking opportunities. Depending on whether your primary interest is geology, wildlife viewing, fishing, or just enjoying the scenery, you may find yourself drawn to one part of the state more than any other. Ironically, some of the best opportunities for enjoying the Alaskan wilderness in its true primitive character are found away from established parks and wilderness areas. There are vast expanses of the state that remain within the public domain but have no special land management status, and many of these lands offer scenery and biotic diversity that rival the most famous of the preserves. Alaska offers an infinite array of possible trips for hikers of all ages and ability levels. By seeking out as much information as possible, you will prepare yourself mentally for the opportunities and obstacles that you will encounter.

Land Ownership in Alaska

Alaska has long been viewed as a land of opportunity. It contains a prodigious wealth of natural resources, from the largest oil and gas fields in the United States to thriving saltwater fisheries. Some of these resources—pristine wilderness, intact ecosystems, and breeding grounds for migratory birds—have a value that cannot be measured in dollars and cents. Throughout the history of the state, conflicts between industry and environmentalists have led to the partitioning of Alaska into zones with varying levels of development. The "locking away" of Alaskan wilderness has become a sore spot between the state and the federal government, and has provided fodder for many a barstool debate.

When the United States bought Alaska from the Russians in the 19th century, Americans knew nothing of its abundant resources. Viewed as a barren wasteland, the new territory was dubbed Seward's Folly in honor of the secretary of state who brokered the deal. The gold rush of the 1890s brought thousands of prospectors to Alaska, and some of these men returned with tales of instant wealth. This information did little to sway the opinions of the American public, however, and Alaska was left to the rugged few who chose to call this wilderness home. A strong spirit of individualism still thrives in the Alaskans of today, many of whom believe that the state would be better off as an independent republic.

When Alaska was granted statehood in 1959, the new state government was awarded the right to select 104 million acres of land for its own use. A few state parks were established, but by and large the lands selected by the state were sold to private

Gold dredges like this one between Boundary and Chicken mark sites of former mining activity.

interests in the name of stimulating economic growth. These private landholders in Alaska are very serious about keeping trespassers off their land, so it is wise to honor "Private Property" signs by staying out. Most of the lands that are not posted or fenced are indeed public, however, and are open for your enjoyment.

The federal government still owns and administers about 75 percent of Alaska's land area, and accords it varying levels of protection according to its management status. Park service lands and national wildlife refuges are accorded the highest level of protection, and heavy industry is almost entirely excluded from these areas. National preserves, often closely associated with national parks, allow sport hunting and, in some cases, off-road-vehicle use. Forest service lands are primarily used for timber production, so be prepared to see acres of clearcuts in areas that are easily accessible.

Much of the remaining federal land is administered by the Bureau of Land Management (BLM), which is responsible for federal lands not claimed for other special purposes. Most of the mining activity in Alaska occurs on BLM land, but overall, the mines make up only a tiny percentage of the land area. All federal lands are open for hiking and backpacking except where these activities are expressly prohibited, and provide myriad opportunities for the adventurous traveler.

The Alaska Native Claims Settlement Act (ANCSA) of 1971 granted large blocks of land to newly formed Native corporations. Native lands are strictly private, but permission is sometimes granted to backpackers who contact the offices of the Native corporations. Addresses for all major Native landholders in Alaska are given in in "The Explorer's Directory" at the back of this book. It is wise to check on the status of the land you plan to cross if you are unsure of its ownership.

Canadian Wildlands

Like Alaska, most of the lands in the Yukon and Northwest Territories are held in trust by government agencies. Most wildlands fall into the category of Crown Lands, which are public domain holdings roughly analogous to the lands managed by the US Bureau of Land Management. Territorial forestry and wildlife agencies have jurisdiction over these lands, and can provide useful information to backpackers. Travelers who wish to register their itineraries can do so with the Royal Canadian Mounted Police. National and territorial parks may have more restrictive regulations, and private lands (including Native lands) and active mining claims are closed to public access.

Getting Around

The highway system in Alaska and northern Canada is not as primitive as you might expect. Many major highways are paved, and gravel highways are graded frequently and constructed so that speeds of 50 miles per hour can usually be maintained. Nevertheless, potholes can be a problem, and sharp gravel has accounted for many a flat tire. If you'll be doing a lot of driving on the gravel highways, you'd be well advised to carry two spare tires instead of one, just as a precaution. Nothing is cheap in Alaska, and this is especially true for car repairs and towing.

Paved highways frequently have frost heaves in areas where the road crosses over permafrost. These troublesome deformities get their start when the blacktop warms up during the long summer days, and the heat is transferred to the ground beneath. This causes the permafrost to melt into a wet muck that is not sturdy enough to support the highway. As a result, the road buckles, forming dips and ridges that will test the performance of the best shock absorbers. When you come to a field of frost heaves, reduce your speed so that you can keep your wheels on the road.

Hitchhiking is a legal and fairly reliable method of travel for backpackers. Since there are so few towns along Alaska's highways, chances are good that the next car will be going your way. Still, here are a few hints to increase your success. First of all, try to hitch from long, straight stretches of highway so that you can be seen from a long way off. Stand on a wide spot in the shoulder so that a car can get off the road safely to pick you up. Display a sign with your destination written on it in large block letters; this will help you get picked up faster. Once you do, consider offering the driver money for gas. This will make drivers more likely to pick up the next hitchhiker they see. Above all, keep safety—both yours and the driver's—in mind at all times. Do not accept rides from drivers who have been drinking or otherwise seem dangerous, and avoid activities that the driver might consider suspicious. Use good judgment; it is unsafe for females to hitchhike alone, and all travelers should avoid hitchhiking at night.

Most of the islands and fjords of southeastern Alaska cannot be reached by road. Instead, the oceangoing ferryliners of the Alaska Marine Highway system shuttle people and vehicles among the numerous populated islands and port towns dotting this region, known as the Inside Passage. Ferry rates are generally highest during the summer. You can use this system to get your car to Alaska as well. Popular jumping-off points are Seattle, Washington, and Prince Rupert, British Columbia. The ferry extends all the way to Haines, Alaska, from which a highway runs north to meet the Alcan in the Yukon. A second network runs throughout Prince William Sound, and ferries also serve Kodiak Island.

Three-quarters of Alaska is not accessible by road, and aircraft have become the transportation of choice for travelers destined for the bush. Major flights service Anchorage and Fairbanks daily, and smaller scheduled flights also service many small bush towns on a regular basis. Scheduled flights and mail planes are substantially cheaper than chartering your own aircraft. Bush pilots provide air-taxi service to many remote locations; if you opt for such service, make sure you bring plenty of cash. As this book went to press, the average fee for a charter aircraft was $250 per flying hour. This can be split up among a group, but remember that larger planes cost more per hour to charter. Float-planes and flying boats can land on most reasonably large lakes, while small aircraft with doughnut-shaped tundra tires can make landings on gravel bars and tundra terraces.

Alaska by Regions

Alaska has almost half the land area of the rest of the United States combined. Imagine traveling from San Diego to Atlanta, and you'll have grasped the approximate east-west span of this great land. Alaska can be broadly divided into a number of topographically distinct regions, each of which has its own characteristic vegetation and weather patterns.

Southeast Alaska is defined by water. The thousand-mile-long stretch of the Inside Passage provides the most accessible routes through this region's rugged mountains and forested fjords. Tlingit and Haida still inhabit quaint bayside villages overlooked by the totem poles of their ancestors. Fair weather is a rarity here, and you can expect to be rained on frequently. Early explorer Addison Powell remarked that "a prospector who visits these mountains should bring a photograph of the sun with him, as well as a diving suit." Because of the difficulty involved in getting around, southeast Alaska is better suited to sea-kayaking than it is to hiking. Waterborne travelers can gain access to myriad trails on the islands and mainland that afford good day-hiking opportunities. Check first at the local US Forest Service office for current trail conditions.

South-central Alaska is a diverse land of moderate rainfall and pleasant climate. The long days of summer make the Matanuska Valley the breadbasket of Alaska, and oversized fruits and vegetables are routinely produced there. Intermittent rain squalls are the rule along the coast, while the broad valleys farther inland typically enjoy sunnier weather. Craggy ranges line the valleys, with peaks that rise well above the timberline. Dense brush is prevalent at lower elevations, and a limited system of trails provides the best option for accessing the high country. Deep winter snows provide the moisture needed to maintain the region's lush vegetation.

The Alaska Peninsula and Aleutian Islands comprise a bleak, stark land with few trees and sparse wildlife. Born of a chain of volcanoes, the Aleutians still experience volcanic upheavals on a regular basis. Access is limited to plane and boat, as no roads connect this remote region with the rest of Alaska. The weather here can be notably foul, with rainstorms being the rule rather than the exception. Winters are relatively mild, with frequent rains and wet snow.

The Copper River Basin is tucked between the Alaska Range to the north and the Wrangell Mountains to the east. A broad, forested bowl, the Copper River Basin often experiences sunny weather even when the surrounding mountains are veiled in clouds. Remote from the larger towns but still accessible by highway, this region is sparsely populated, but contains a rich diversity of wildlife.

The interior of Alaska extends along the great Yukon Basin from the Yukon border west to the Bering Sea. Miles and miles of uninterrupted boreal forest characterize the region, which is also known for its low hills mantled in loess, or windblown glacial dust. The entire region remained unglaciated during the ice ages, and the then arid grasslands gave refuge to a rich assemblage of giant mammals, from woolly mammoths to sabertoothed cats. In the present day, wildlife is relatively sparse and difficult to view. The weather in the interior is predictably dry, with hot summer temperatures occasionally reaching 90 degrees Fahrenheit.

Alaska's vast Arctic encompasses a stark and beautiful landscape populated by animals specially adapted to life in the frigid North. The treeless tundra of the North Slope is pockmarked with lakes and ponds that harbor breeding populations of waterfowl. Huge herds of caribou migrate hundreds of miles to breed along the barren coast of the Arctic Ocean. The long winters and stormy summers provide little chance for the ground to thaw, and, as a result, permafrost lurks only inches below the surface of the soil.

Areas of Special Interest

The Brooks Range. The Brooks Range is Alaskan wilderness at its best. This untrammeled wilderness has no trails, but is criss-crossed by a network of broad, glacier-carved valleys that interlink at low passes. Its wild, clear rivers host an abundance of char and grayling. The mountains themselves are characterized by steep rock pinnacles and broad glacial valleys. Those rivers and peaks that are named at all sport Inuit monikers like Doonerak and Nunamiut. Dall sheep and grizzly bears are commonly seen, along with the occasional caribou, Arctic fox, and the ubiquitous Arctic ground squirrel. There are no trails up here, so bring your map and compass. The valley bottoms of the southern slope are filled with spruce and brush, which makes for rough going. The north side of the divide has open tundra, and hiking is easy if you can avoid the tussock tundra. Access is limited to the rough gravel surface of the Dalton Highway (a 9-hour drive from Fairbanks) and to air travel. Commercial flights provide affordable service to Anaktuvuk Pass on the north slope of Gates of the Arctic National Park; for a steeper price, bush pilots out of Fairbanks and Bettles will fly you into more remote locations. The villages of Anaktuvuk Pass and Coldfoot offer scant provisions at high prices; stock up on what you need before you leave civilization. The western half of the range is administered under the auspices of the National Park Service, while the dramatic eastern side falls within the Arctic National Wildlife Refuge.

The White Mountains. Long a secret escape for native Fair-banksans, the White Mountains provide wilderness hiking opportunities just north of town. The Whites are characterized by moderately steep, forested ridges topped with tundra. Marshy black spruce permafrost typifies the valley bottoms and north-facing slopes. Trails into the White Mountains are most suitable for backpacking and extended trips, because they take a while to get where they're going! Expect to see lots of ptarmigan, a few black or grizzly bears, and moose along the way. The

Bureau of Land Management (BLM) maintains six cabins in this area for public use (reservations and a small fee are required). The White Mountains can be reached via the Elliot or Steese Highways and are a 1-hour drive north of Fairbanks.

Chena State Recreation Area. This is a pleasant spot in the foothills north of Fairbanks. Developed trails are available for day hikes (Angel Rock, the Granite Tors) or extended backpacks (Ester Dome). This forested country is known for its geological oddities, the granite towers or *tors* that protrude from ridgetops like silent sentinels. Rock climbers like the solid granite that is found in this neck of the woods, while canoeists can find pleasant paddling on the waters of the Chena River. This area is reached by traveling about 40 miles north of Fairbanks on the Chena Hot Springs Road, a paved thoroughfare that departs from the Steese Highway just outside Fairbanks. The privately owned hot springs at the end of the road have been developed into a resort.

Denali National Park. The crown jewel in the Alaskan wilderness system, Denali National Park covers a huge swath of the Alaska Range between Fairbanks and Anchorage. This park was originally established to protect wildlife populations from overhunting, and is home to one of the most spectacular arrays of fauna in the world. Dall sheep, grizzly bears, caribou, moose, and gray wolves are all commonly seen. The two peaks of Denali, at over 20,000 feet, constitute the tallest mountain in North America (some folks from the lower 48 still insist on calling it Mount McKinley). This magnificent mountain provides a dazzling backdrop for verdant expanses of Arctic tundra (although it often hides behind a veil of clouds).

It takes 2 hours from Fairbanks or 4 from Anchorage to drive the paved Parks Highway to Denali National Park. There are several lodges at the entrance, with limited opportunities to purchase provisions. Expect resort prices. The park road is closed to public traffic beyond the Savage River, but shuttle bus service provides access into the interior of the park for a steep fee.

Looking toward Indian Peak from K'esugi Ridge, Denali State Park

Trails are the exception in here; backcountry users are expected to make their own way across the tundra with as little impact as possible. Denali has a sophisticated backpacking permit system that limits the number of users in each drainage to preserve the wilderness experience for all. (It does not yet apply to day hikers.) Get to the visitor center early in the morning so you can have the greatest chance of getting your first choice for a backpacking destination. Bear-resistant food containers are mandatory for backcountry users, and are available free of charge from the visitor center.

Denali State Park. A smaller cousin to Denali National Park, this state-managed area is located 50 miles south of its larger relative on the Parks Highway. This area is too brushy for bushwhacking, but does boast a few maintained trails, featuring one 36-miler that travels along the crest of K'esugi Ridge with a spectacular view of Denali to the west on a clear day. The far western portion of the park can be reached via a 3-hour drive on the Petersville Road if you have four-wheel drive. Fishing is fairly good in the streams of this park, with runs of red, pink, and silver salmon arriving in mid- to late summer, and a few resident rainbows providing fishing throughout the year.

The Denali Highway. This gravel highway makes its way through miles of untrammeled BLM land in the heart of the Alaska Range, providing many opportunities for the adventurous backpacker. It begins midway between Fairbanks and Anchorage on the Parks Highway (about 3½ hours from each), and reaches its endpoint an hour's drive south of Delta Junction. Habitats vary from spruce bog to open tundra, with dense underbrush along some of the major rivers. The far western part of the highway, near the headwaters of the Susitna River, as well as the MacLaren River area, provide especially pleasant tundra hiking without the crowds associated with some of the more developed parks. Fishing can be good in clear-flowing rivers and streams, and improves as you travel farther from the road.

Hatcher Pass. The former site of one of Alaska's largest gold mines, Hatcher Pass is nestled among the craggy massifs of the Talkeetna Mountains on the Fishhook Road between Palmer and Willow. The area in the immediate vicinity of the pass has several maintained trails for day hikers and backpackers, both at the historical park encompassing the mine site and in the surrounding valleys. Gold panning is allowed here, and pans are available on loan from the visitor center. The alpine tundra in this area provides a wonderful traveling surface, and if you are adventurous, you can find a number of small valleys that have no trails but are nevertheless ideal for exploring on foot. Wildlife is abundant in the high alpine valleys; look among the boulders for the tiny pika, a short-eared relative of the rabbit. Golden eagles nest in the high cliffs, and are often spotted as they soar on the thermals, searching for rodents.

Wrangell–St. Elias National Park. America's largest national park is primitive and undeveloped, and as a result its backcountry receives few tourists. The park borders on Kluane National Park in the Yukon, and shares the icy St. Elias massif with our Canadian neighbors. The snowy summits of the Wrangell Mountains rise from the black spruce bogs of the Copper River Basin, and glaciers descend from the frigid heights to the valleys below. Surrounding the park are national preserve lands, in which hunting and off-road vehicles are allowed. The park is a 5-hour drive from Anchorage on good paved highways. Towns along its fringes are small and typically have country stores that stock a limited offering of camping provisions.

The park's northern section is accessible via a gravel road that runs from Slana, on the Tok Cutoff Highway, deep into the park to the tiny cluster of buildings called Nabesna, nestled among the mountains. The road is passable to all cars during dry periods, but it does ford several creeks that swell and become impassable to all but four-wheel drives following heavy rains. There are a number of primitive trails that run from this road into the surrounding backcountry, and the landscape is also well suited to bushwhacking.

In the south, the Edgerton Highway runs to Chitina, where a narrow, primitive gravel road follows an old railway roadbed for 61 miles to the Kennicott River. The road ends at this point, and you must take a hand-powered aerial tram over the river to reach the settlement of McCarthy. The well-preserved buildings of the old Kennecott copper mine lie just 4 miles north of town, a ghostly reminder of the boomtown days of the turn of the century. There are no maintained trails in the southern part of the park, but bushwhacking is possible along glacial moraines and up creek valleys. Park rangers may recommend a number of routes for backpackers desiring extended trips. Air-taxi and guide services in McCarthy also provide access to more remote (and more readily traversable) parts of the park.

The Chugach Mountains. Chugach National Forest, the Kenai National Wildlife Refuge, and the state of Alaska have provided a network of trails in the Chugach and Kenai Mountains for those of the backpacking persuasion who prefer to tread the

Rainbow Lake is among a multitude of beautiful lakes nestled among the Kenai Mountains.

beaten path. Trails from the fringes of Anchorage ascend steeply into the high country of Chugach State Park, sparing users the effort of bushwhacking through the lower elevations on their way to the alpine tundra. On the Kenai Peninsula, an extensive network of trails provides access to subalpine lakes and moose-filled meadows at the foot of snow-clad mountains. The Resurrection Trail, which runs from the village of Hope to the city of Seward, provides a great route for extended trips, with forest service cabins (nominal charge, advance reservations required) provided along the way. During his early exploration of this area in 1899, Lieutenant John Herron noted that "the mountains are high and their steep sides from timberline down are covered with timber, brush, fallen trees, rocks, and ravines, making travel very annoying." Not much has changed in 100 years, and thus bushwhacking is not recommended in this area.

Kenai Fjords National Park and Vicinity. Although Kenai Fjords National Park is most easily accessed by boat, there are some opportunities for those of us who are limited to shoe leather as a means of transportation. The Exit Glacier area features day hikes of varying intensity, most notably the Harding Icefield trail, which runs beside Exit Glacier to the Harding Icefield. The icefield itself is traversable on foot or (preferably) cross-country skis for adventurous souls who take the time to familiarize themselves with the hazards of glacier travel. Major crevasses are well marked on topographic maps and can be avoided if some care is taken.

The park has its headquarters just outside of Seward, which is a 4-hour drive from Anchorage. Seward has outlets for camping and fishing gear, as well as full-service grocery stores. Near Seward, primitive, unmaintained trails run west up Mount Marathon, a strenuous day hike that rewards the successful with a sweeping view of Resurrection Bay. Another trail runs southward along the bayshore, eventually reaching the old World War II coastal defense installation on Caines Head, a popular destination for backpackers. Much of this route is submerged during high tides; consult local tide tables before setting out.

Kachemak Bay State Park. This wilderness gem is set across Kachemak Bay from Homer on the southern tip of the Kenai Peninsula (a 4-hour drive from Anchorage). All services are offered in Homer; there are none in the park itself, which is accessible only by boat or airplane. At the time of this writing, a round trip to the park by water taxi cost $50 and included a tour of the seabird rookeries at Gull Island. In the park, there is an extensive and well-maintained trail system around Halibut Cove, featuring trails that access spectacular glaciers, climb high onto alpine ridges and mountaintops, and wind along forested coves. Many of the trails along the coast require some hiking below the high-tide line; appropriate precautions should be taken. The eastern corner of the park is a wilderness without trails, and provides a challenge for even the experienced backcountry traveler.

The Chilkoot Trail. This historic gold rush route crosses one of only three ice-free passages between the shores of the

Alaskan panhandle and the old goldfields of the Klondike. The easiest access is via the ferry, but a paved highway also connects Skagway with the Alaska Highway near Whitehorse, Yukon. A railway parallels the route to offer a scenic and unusual way to get back to your starting point. Because this route crosses the border with Canada, all backpackers must first clear customs. Due to the popularity of this route, travelers should expect crowds of fellow hikers.

The trek begins in the coastal rainforest near Skagway, climbs through the stark boulder fields and windswept tundra of Chilkoot Pass, and then passes into the boreal forest of the Canadian interior. Along the way, travelers may encounter artifacts cast aside by gold rush prospectors. The trail is 33 miles in length, and takes from 3 to 5 days to complete. It is administered by the National Park Service, with permits available at the Skagway visitor center. Travelers planning to traverse this rugged and often muddy route should gather information well in advance. The pass may be snowbound late into summer, so be sure to check the prevailing conditions before you go.

Tongass National Forest. This forest encompasses the entire length of southeast Alaska, including the archipelago that guards the Inside Passage. It has an extensive trail system covering hundreds of miles, much of which is only accessible by boat. The coastal forests give way to icebound peaks as you move inland, and glaciers pour down into the fjords to meet the sea. The country is dominated by coastal rainforest in areas that have not been clearcut; Sitka spruce, hemlock, and cedar are the dominant tree species. Coastal brown bears are quite abundant in some locales, and they feed on the vigorous runs of salmon that spawn in the small streams of the islands. Bald eagles may also be spotted at the height of these runs. Blacktail deer and timber wolves are also present in some locations, although the thick timber and brush make them difficult to spot. The higher crags are inhabited by mountain goats. Perhaps the most outstanding wildlife found here are marine mammals: Killer whales, humpback whales, seals, and sea otters are all commonly seen along the coast. The larger towns can be reached via the ferry system, and water- and air taxis offer service to the more remote trailheads. Stock up on provisions in Juneau, Ketchikan, or Sitka.

Katmai National Park. This sprawling expanse of snow-clad volcanoes and coastal brushlands occupies the base of the Alaska Peninsula. It can be reached by scheduled airline service from Anchorage to King Salmon, and by charter plane from there. Expect to find limited provisions and high prices in King Salmon, because most items arrive by air freight. The area is noted for its abundance of brown bears and caribou and boasts the largest specimens of moose in the world. Recent volcanism is evident in the Valley of Ten Thousand Smokes, a barren and broken land of fumaroles and volcanic ash. The alpine country of the higher mountains is well suited to backpacking, although the low country is choked with thickets of willow.

The Canadian Arctic

Canada's Arctic regions provide a vast and unspoiled wonderland for wilderness travelers. There are a few national parks, but most of the land area is held in the public domain. These public lands are called Crown Lands, and are open to most kinds of motorless recreation. The road system in the southern Yukon is well developed and mostly paved, but the roads that run northward to the Northwest Territories are typically gravel and offer limited services along the way. Travelers who enter Canada from the United States will have to pass through customs. In general, handguns and fresh produce cannot be brought into Canada, and all alcohol must be declared at the border. Be sure to have proper identification, vehicle registration and insurance, and enough cash on hand to see you through any emergency that may arise. Customs agents are constantly on the lookout for child abductions, so make sure that you have proper identification for any children you bring along. Canadians are fiercely proud of their national heritage, and have distinctive customs that differ from those found in the United States.

Kluane National Park (Yukon Territories). Just across the border from Wrangell–St. Elias National Park, the Kluane *(kloo-AH-nee)* country forms the other half of a Biosphere Reserve, recognized by the United Nations for its outstanding ecological importance. The inner peaks are locked in ice and snow, and it is difficult to penetrate them very far without resorting to glacier travel. But outer ranges like the Auriol Mountains provide ample hiking opportunities for the adventurous, and feature abundant snowfields and rock glaciers. The lowland forests here are composed primarily of lodgepole pine, which dominates the vegetation of the Canadian Rockies farther to the south, and is difficult to travel through due to blowdowns. River valleys tend to be overgrown with brush and filled with bears, so proceed with caution in these areas. Primitive travel routes are recommended by a helpful staff at the visitor center in Haines Junction. The Kluane can be reached on the Alaska Highway, which is about 150 bumpy miles from the Alaskan border. Folks who are flying north will find it an easy 2-hour drive from the capital city of Whitehorse.

This sweeping tundra vista characterizes the Ogilvie Mountains of the central Yukon.

Ogilvie Mountains (Yukon). The Ogilvie Mountains lie 30 miles north of Dawson City on the gravel Dempster Highway. As you travel northward, the trees fall away, leaving you lost in the haunting emptiness of tundra. These mountains are of sedimentary origin and have a gentle aspect. The Tombstone Mountains are an igneous intrusion into the Ogilvies, and are highlighted by stark monoliths of granite that thrust skyward from tundra-clad bases. The tundra is brushy and difficult to penetrate on the south side of the range, while north of the Klondike River divide it is open and quite boggy in places. This area is a major winter range of the Porcupine caribou herd, as well as an all-season home to a few resident caribou. It is a 2-day trip to reach these spectacular pinnacles, along primitive and unmaintained trails. The rest of the Ogilvie Mountains provide trail-free tundra hiking. Getting around is easy once you decide where to go, but stick to the slopes to avoid the tussock tundra that covers the valley floors.

The Richardson Mountains (Yukon/Northwest Territories). This tundra-clad range rises along the border between the Yukon and Northwest Territories, and can be accessed from Dawson City via a long day's drive on the Dempster Highway. This range has never been glaciated, and its sedimentary peaks have been reduced to graceful curves by the relentless action of frost shattering. It offers good hiking across well-drained tundra, with intriguing permafrost features like stone nets and solifluction terraces that provide an ever-changing natural history lesson.

Canol Road (Northwest Territories). During World War II, this road and its associated pipeline were punched through the wilderness of the Yukon and Northwest Territories to reach the oil fields at Norman Wells. North of Macmillan Pass on the Yukon/Northwest Territories border, the road has been left to the elements and is now a heritage trail. It takes a long day of driving on gravel highways to reach this point from Whitehorse in the Yukon. The abandoned roadway makes a challenging route for backpackers and mountain bikers, with a few river crossings where the bridges have been washed out by floods. Watch for broken-down trucks and abandoned Quonset huts left over from the construction period.

Nahanni National Park (Northwest Territories). This remote wilderness park protects a corridor around the scenic South Nahanni River. This river flows from the spectacular Mackenzie Mountains out through the Ram Plateau, and features Rabbitkettle Hot Springs and Virginia Falls, a cascade twice as tall as Niagara Falls. Most travelers see the park on float trips that can last up to 14 days. There are some fine day-hiking opportunities along side canyons though, and the Mackenzie Mountains have open tundra that offers spectacular backpacking possibilities. Charter flights from Fort Nelson, British Columbia, and Fort Liard and Fort Simpson, Northwest Territories, provide access to Rabbitkettle Lake and Virginia Falls.

Ivvavik National Park (Yukon). This park was set aside in conjunction with the adjacent Arctic National Wildlife Refuge in Alaska to protect the calving grounds of the Porcupine caribou herd. It spans the Arctic Coastal Plains and the British Mountains, and offers hiking terrain similar to that found in the Brooks Range. The Firth River flows through the park to the Arctic Ocean, providing one of the most outstanding river trips in the Arctic. Charter planes from Inuvik, Northwest Territories, provide access to the park.

Aulavik National Park (Northwest Territories). This new park is located on Banks Island, home to the highest concentration of muskox in the world. Most visitors come to canoe the Thomsen River, an Arctic waterway of sheer bluffs, deep canyons, and eroded badlands. The open tundra of the uplands has excellent potential for backpacking expeditions. The park can be accessed by charter flight from Inuvik.

3 Gearing Up for Alaska

THE equipment that you carry on your back can make the difference between a miserable slog and an unforgettable trip. Your comfort level is of utmost importance, because discomfort has a tendency to work its way into the brain, preempting more pleasurable thoughts. You should select your equipment with an eye to your comfort; nature itself will give you plenty of chances to rough it without any help from faulty or inadequate gear.

Many expeditions start off with a last-minute mad scramble to grab all the gear and get out the door. With this in mind, plan ahead and make a list of all of the things you will need for your trip ahead of time, and double-check while your hiking buddies are scrambling around looking for the gloves they last saw in February. I like to lay all of my stuff out on the floor and sort through it visually; this prevents important items being left behind. Take a little extra time to double-check, because if you find out later that you forgot something it will be too late. This chapter contains a detailed discussion of the pros and cons of various backpacking equipment, with an eye toward helping you select the gear that will be most useful in the Alaskan wilds.

Dressing in Layers

If you've done a lot of backpacking, you are probably well acquainted with the idea of dressing in layers. Extra clothes mean extra weight, and yet you must be prepared for hot and freezing weather alike. Versatility is the name of the game, and the layering approach allows you a flexible array of clothing choices to match changing weather conditions. Ideally, you'd like to have the appropriate clothing for days of 90 degrees Fahrenheit and zero-degree mornings, with a capability to withstand wind, freezing rain, and snow.

Let's start with undergarments. You should pack some lightweight, brief undergarments for warm weather, and long underwear to use as a base garment in colder situations. Polypropylene (polypro) and other synthetics provide warmth and tend to wick perspiration away from the skin, where it can make you damp and clammy. For warmth and comfort, synthetic-wool combinations are even better. Avoid using cotton, as it will retain the water next to your skin, sapping you of heat.

Lots of people backpack in blue jeans, probably because that's what we're used to wearing on a day-to-day basis. But for backpacking, blue jeans are a pretty poor choice. Their fabric is rather heavy, and when they get wet, they stay that way for days. Water has an incredible capacity for absorbing heat, and several pounds of it next to your skin can cool you off in a big hurry. If you bring pants along, try to bring nylon wind pants or baggy synthetic blends that will dry off quickly. I generally do not bring pants along at all; a pair of walking shorts to wear over my longjohns and rain pants to keep off the wind seem to suffice under most conditions. When cold weather is expected, synthetic pile or wool pants can keep your legs wonderfully warm.

Your choice of shirts should be functional above all else. I like to bring along a mixture of lightweight T-shirts for warm weather and turtlenecks for layering when it's cooler. You can get by with only a couple of shirts for long trips; you're not going to find any laundry facilities in the backcountry anyway, so don't be afraid to get them dirty. Do make sure that you have enough of them so that you always have something warm and dry to change into when you get to camp.

It is absolutely essential to bring along a thick, warm top to wear over your shirt to keep you insulated when the temperature drops below freezing. Your chest and abdomen form the core of heat production, and a loss of body core temperature can lead to hypothermia. Your top should be the thermal equivalent of a medium-weight coat, and should repel water and dry off quickly. For years, I have brought a heavy-weight wool commando sweater on every trip I have taken into the woods, and it has kept me warm in all types of weather. Synthetic fleece pullovers and jackets are also a good choice.

Stay away from clothing insulated by goose down. As soon as it gets wet, down sticks together and loses its *loft,* which is the warm barrier of air trapped between the fibers that insulates against the cold. As a result, a wet down vest or jacket is no help at all against the cold.

You can increase your comfort immeasurably during cold weather by bringing along some warm coverings for your extremities. Most of the heat that you lose goes out through your head and neck, so a lightweight wool or polypro hat is a good thing to have along. The *balaclava*—which is like a big sock for your head with a hole for your face—is a good design because it keeps your neck warm when rolled down. Some lightweight wool or polypro gloves will keep your fingers warm and functional when the temperature starts dropping. If you will be traveling during hunting season, it is wise to bring along a blaze-orange hat or other garment so that hunters can see that you are not a game animal.

Socks are the most important and often the most neglected part of a hiker's wardrobe. Nothing beats a good pair of wool socks, which will absorb some of the shock of walking and keep your feet warm even when wet. There are some new synthetic fabrics that are now being used for hiking socks; in my experience they do not keep your feet as dry as wool. Make sure that your socks are shaped for maximum comfort. Tube socks with no shaped heel bunch up at the top of the foot and wear out quickly in the heel. Many hikers like to wear ultrathin silk or polypro sock liners over their feet in order to minimize blister-causing friction as well as to draw water away from the skin. Bring a pair of socks for every day you will be out in the backcountry, up to three pairs. This way, if it rains the entire time, you can still rotate the socks that you wear so that you always have a dry pair to put on at the end of a long day.

Since the weather in Alaska is so unpredictable, you should expect to be rained on each time you go out on a trip. Even if the rain is not falling hard enough to get you wet, the vegetation growing along your path will soak you to the bone if you don't wear proper raingear. In other parts of the country, you might get away with a rain poncho, but up in Alaska you'll need a good quality, lightweight rain parka and pants. Gore-Tex is popular with many hikers for its breatheability, but it will never keep you dry in a steady downpour. I prefer rubber-treated nylon rainwear, which is available at most sporting goods stores for a reasonable price. If you can find rain pants with zippers all the way up the outside of both legs, grab them: They can be unzipped to release heat buildup in your legs. You will probably have to slow your hiking pace when wearing a rain suit, because these suits are great insulators and if you are really exerting yourself, perspiration will soak you from the inside.

Gaiters are nice luxury items used by many experienced backpackers. They fit over your boot tops to protect you from rain, snow, or rocks that would otherwise fall into your boot tops. You can also use them in conjunction with shorts when hiking in the rain; your legs will get wet but will not overheat as they might if you were wearing rain pants.

Footwear

There are many different ideas about what constitutes proper footwear for hiking in Alaska. The right solution to your footwear needs depends upon where you'll be hiking. The priorities in this department are good traction, comfort, and dry feet, not necessarily in that order. Ankle support is also a quality to look for, especially if you have a history of weak joints. Your feet are the most important backpacking equipment you have, so it is important to keep them in top condition.

Breakup boots are knee-high rubber boots that are commonly used by hunters and biologists in the wetter areas of the state. They come in insulated and uninsulated varieties, and range in price from $10 to $80. In tussock tundra and other swampy environments, breakup boots will keep your feet dry when nothing else will. They are also great for fording small streams without getting your feet wet. They are, however, horribly uncomfortable to walk in, especially with weight on your back. If you use them, expect lots of twigs in your socks and try to find some sort of insoles or arch supports, because these boots are not well designed to accommodate the architecture of your foot.

Heavy-weight mountaineering boots, with their steel-shanked soles and heavy leather uppers, were once popular with backpackers in Alaska. They are heavy and clunky, and their soles have too little flex to make hiking very easy. Stay away from these unless you will be doing technical mountaineering on your trip, where the stiff soles will allow you to cling to narrow ledges above death-defying dropoffs. They also have specially designed soles that can accept crampons.

In the 1980s, the Hi-tec Corporation invented a series of lightweight hiking boots patterned after running shoes, and they were so popular that most boot companies now sell their own imitations. These boots generally have good solid soles, with cloth and leather uppers, and some of them even have Gore-Tex liners for waterproofing. But even the ones with Gore-Tex won't keep your feet dry for long. If you are prepared to hike around with soaked feet all day, these boots are an acceptable choice. Otherwise, look for something more substantial.

Manufacturers of hiking boots are also incorporating modern technology into the traditional leather hiking boot. Look for flexible lug soles for traction, medium-height leather uppers, and solid stitching. The leather will probably need to be waterproofed from time to time; there are a number of waxes and oils, both natural and synthetic, that are currently on the market to achieve this end. Most boots come with information on which waterproofing compound to use. However, just having waterproof boots will not guarantee you dry feet, because water will frequently be above boot-top level in boggy habitats.

Shoe-pacs feature rubber lowers and leather uppers, and are commonly used in cold weather. If you're using shoe-pacs, your feet will stay dry under most circumstances. However, they do not breathe and will bathe your feet in sweat on warm days.

Bunny boots are heavy, inflatable-rubber affairs developed by the military for winter combat in Arctic conditions. They will keep your feet warm when nothing else will. If you plan to be active, though, bunny boots will quickly fill up with sweat.

If there are river and stream crossings on your itinerary, you might consider bring along a pair of lightweight shoes specifically to wear in the water. River sandals work well, as do canvas sneakers. These extra shoes can double as camp moccasins to give your feet a break from hiking boots at the end of the day. If you are worried about the weight involved in carrying extra shoes, you can hike in neoprene socks and leave your hiking boots on in the water. This option will give you the most stable footing, and will keep your feet warm (although they will be soggy all of the time).

Backpacks

The raging debate over the virtues of internal- versus external-frame packs seems to have settled down, and these days most backpackers go for the internal-frame variety. To be sure, internal-frame packs do tend to move with your body, and thus are a better choice for scrambling around on rock faces. The same logic holds for cross-country skiing, where an external-frame pack will ride on your back with all the grace and comfort of a sheet of plywood. For backpacking, however, an external-frame pack with a good hip belt will be as comfortable as an internal-frame pack, and may be less costly.

There are certain characteristics that you should look for in a backpack, regardless of style. First and foremost, the pack should be comfortable—this means a well-padded hip belt and comfortable straps that will adjust to accommodate a variety of loads. If you are buying an external-frame pack, be sure that the frame fits the contours of your back. Most internal-frame packs have flexible stays that can be bent for this purpose. Extra belt loops and straps that allow you to tie gear to the outside increase the capacity of the pack. A good pack has lots of external pockets that allow you to keep small items handy while you're on the trail. For the main compartment, I prefer the top-loading variety, but packs that zip open in the back have just as many proponents. If you plan to take trips of more than 3 days' duration, you'll need a pack with at least 5000 cubic inches of carrying capacity. Look for a pack with heavy-duty packcloth on the bottom, as this material resists wear much better than lighter weight nylons. If you can afford it, it is also wise to purchase a rain cover for your pack, because while most backpacks are water-resistant, they cannot hold out the moisture during a steady downpour.

Tents

A good tent is your insurance policy against foul weather. A strong tent will stay up during windstorms, provide a barrier against marauding critters, and keep you dry through all types of weather. Most modern tents have a waterproof bottom of heavy-duty nylon and a thin, breatheable upper that allows water vapor to escape during the night. A waterproof rainfly covers the whole show, keeping the elements out and allowing water vapor to condense outside the tent, where it cannot drip on you the following morning. Expedition-quality tents may also have an optional vestibule, which is an extension of the fly that provides a sheltered area for cooking and gear storage.

When looking for a tent that will stand up to Alaskan weather, keep a few considerations in mind. You will be carrying the tent on your back, so the lighter the tent the better. The whole tent, including stakes and poles, should weigh no more than 12 pounds for a two-person tent or 15 pounds for a four-person tent. The tent should be freestanding, which means that it will stay up even after all the stakes have been pulled. This feature allows you to set up camp in rocky or sandy areas, where getting stakes to hold can be a problem. Four-season tents are not

A good backpack will put the wieght of your load on your hips, not your shoulders.

only sturdily built to keep you absolutely dry in the worst storm, but they also retain warmth much better than conventional tents. They tend to be quite expensive, however, and may not be a practical purchase if you don't do a lot of camping.

A final consideration is tent color. Select an earth-toned tent that blends into the landscape. Bright-colored tents are an eyesore on the open tundra, and will detract from the wilderness experience of other visitors in the area.

Some tent designs are better than others. By far the best design for a backpacking tent is the geodesic dome (and its oblong variants), in which a network of interlocking poles supports the dome-shaped roof. Dome tents are always freestanding, and their shape sheds the wind easily, making them stable during a storm. Dome tents with four or more poles are the most stable. Look for an interlocking geodesic shape, where the poles intersect at numerous points to stabilize each other. If the poles all cross at the center, the tent will be less sturdy. Another design features a tall, flexible hoop above the entrance and another smaller hoop above the foot of the tent. This design may be freestanding, or may be held erect by tension when it is staked down. A third variety is the A-frame or pup tent. Once very popular, most of these tents are held aloft by guy lines and can be counted on to fold up during heavy weather.

Tents must be given special care in order to ensure that they remain waterproof. For most tents, it is necessary to seal all of the seams in the floor and the fly with a special sealing compound every couple of years. Some backpackers like to bring along a piece of plastic sheeting to serve as a ground cloth in wet terrain. Never use any kind of open flame or very hot instrument inside your tent, because the nylon is prone to melting if exposed to high temperatures. And always try to keep your tent dry when it is not in use, because a wet tent is an ideal surface for smelly mildew, which forms ugly stains and may weaken the fabric.

Sleeping Bags and Pads

To a large extent, how well you sleep in the Alaskan outdoors will depend on your choice of a sleeping bag and pad. Sleeping bags should be comfort-rated down to at least 20 degrees, and a bag rated to 10 degrees is even better. Summer bags rated at 30 degrees or higher will not keep you warm if a coldfront blows in, and bags rated for zero degrees or colder will cook you if the temperature is much above freezing. Besides the bag's warmth, consider its lightness: Try to find a bag that is light in weight and stuffs down to a small size when packed. If your sleeping bag comes with a nylon stuff-sack, you can fill the empty sack with soft clothing at night and use it as a pillow.

Materials used in the construction of sleeping bags have benefited from technological advances in the field of chemistry. New fiber-fills like Quallofil and PolarGuard provide outstanding loft for comparatively little weight. Down is also a lightweight fill with good insulating qualities, but down loses its insulating ability when wet and thus is not appropriate for backpacking in Alaska. When choosing a bag, look for offset construction, in which seams do not go all the way through the bag. A draft collar in the neck area and an insulated flap for the zipper will help keep out the cold, too.

There are several types of sleeping bags to choose from, and the right sleeping bag for you depends on your personal taste and budget. Mummy bags are form fitting, and feature a hood with a drawstring that can be pulled tight to create a cocoon of warmth. Mummy bags can be quite restrictive, however, despite their excellent warmth-to-weight ratio. A variant of the mummy bag is the modified mummy, which sports a slightly wider taper for freer movement inside the bag. These bags also feature hoods with a drawstring that can be pulled tight to seal out the cold. Traditional, square bags are inexpensive, but are generally heavy and may not be sufficiently warm. Couples who backpack might take advantage of the capability of many sleeping bags to zip together, forming a warm double bag for two.

The addition of a sleeping pad to your camping gear will increase your nighttime comfort immeasurably. Sleeping pads come in short lengths (shoulders to hips), and full-length ones (head to toe). A new generation of sleeping pads combines soft foam with an inflatable shell. These inflatable pads are wonderful to sleep on, but can become a real pain if they develop leaks. Closed-cell foam pads have an excellent capacity for insulating you from the cold ground, but are rather hard and uncomfortable. Open-cell waffle foam is great for comfort, but provides little protection from the cold. You can have the best of both worlds by purchasing a pad that has both types of foam sealed together to form a single pad.

Cooking Gear

Because firewood is often scarce and campfires are not allowed in many places, the backpacking stove has become standard issue among folks who like to spend the night in the backcountry. Most run on white gas, which can be purchased by the gallon at most sporting goods stores. A few of the fancier ones burn everything from kerosene to unleaded gas. Characteristics to look for in a stove are lightness of weight, dependability, and average boiling time, which is the amount of time the stove takes to boil water at sea level. If you can get a special windscreen to go with your stove, bring it along, as it will dramatically decrease your frustration (and speed up the cooking).

I recommend the old Optimus climber's stove, because it is light in weight, does not require pumping, and is self-cleaning. Coleman and MSR also make good backpacking stoves, but they clog up from time to time and must be taken apart and cleaned. There are stoves on the market that can burn almost any type of fuel, but most burn only white gas. The advantage of having the capacity to burn alternative fuels is a rather dubious one, unless you plan to do some traveling to preindustrial countries. Stay away from propane-fueled stoves if you can, because the fuel canisters cannot be refilled and thus fuel costs can be quite high.

You will also need a fuel container. Most are made of aluminum, and some are coated with a special paint that prevents them from rubbing aluminum dust onto everything that they touch. A fuel bottle with 250 milliliters of capacity should be more than enough for most short trips. Special pour-spout lids are also available for these fuel containers, and are much easier to use (although slightly more expensive) than a plastic funnel. To light your stove, bring along a cigarette lighter or waterproof matches. Do not rely on waterproof containers to keep your matches dry, because if they fail, you will be out of luck.

Your cookware should be light and simple. Aluminum is the most common material, but stainless steel is becoming more available in lighter weights for backpackers. Aluminum is known to flake off into your food in small amounts each time you cook, and has been linked to deterioration of brain function in elderly people. Thus, stainless steel cookware should be your first choice if you can afford it. Some people can get by with just a wide-lipped sierra cup and a spoon, but I prefer to bring a 3-quart pot with a matching sauté pan, and both forks and spoons. There are larger nesting cook sets, complete with plates, that are designed to be used by parties of two or four. If you plan to fry anything, make sure that one of your pans is Teflon-coated; otherwise, whatever you try to fry will inevitably stick to the pan like glue. Finally, a water bag makes a worthy addition to your cooking equipment. For a small amount of added weight, it will allow you to pitch your tent farther from water sources, and alleviate the need for frequent trips to and from the water.

Fueling Your Body

You will eat incredible amounts of food when you are out on the trail. Heavy exercise and the energetic cost of staying warm will combine to give you an appetite you never imagined possible, so it is always a good idea to pack more than you think you will eat. The premium is on lightness of weight when backpacking, so dry foods to which water can be added are the most favorable for backpacking purposes. You will benefit from the fact that everything tastes better when you are camping, so don't worry if you are not a first-rate chef.

Breakfast is the most important meal of the day when you are in the backcountry, and yet the eating habits of Western society have long neglected it. I like to start the day with lots of carbohydrates, which give energy on a sustained basis throughout the day. Alaskan mornings are often quite chilly even at the height of summer, and a hot cereal like rolled oats or wheat farina goes a long way to warm you up. These hot breakfasts are now available in convenient one-serving packets complete with powdered milk and spices. But remember that one serving to a cereal manufacturer means enough to feed a small, inactive child. For people who don't like the hassle of firing up the stove in the morning, cold cereals can be eaten dry to provide a hearty and sustaining breakfast.

Many folks have a hard time imagining what they will bring for lunch on a backpacking trip. After all, the all-American sandwich, a staple of two generations, doesn't pack very well. The solution is in bringing a number of small, snack-style items that combine light weight and high caloric value in a convenient package. Trail mix, also known as *gorp*, is a mixture of fruits, nuts, and grains that makes a good snack food and can be bought in bulk at many food stores. Beef jerky is also a good choice for a lightweight and flavorsome addition to any lunch. Granola bars come in a bewildering array of varieties, and are packaged singly for ease and convenience. And toaster pastries are good sources of sugar for that quick burst of energy when you are running out of momentum. There are also a variety of high-energy bars on the market specifically formulated for the needs of active people. Dried fruit snacks provide sugar and all-important fiber in your diet, and can be added for balance. Even cheese keeps well in these northern climes, but will be a scent attractor in bear country. Remember that variety is the spice of life, and pack a number of different items to keep lunches interesting. You will be carrying all of this food, so you will need to minimize the weight while maximizing the food value (and calories!) of your selection.

A good evening meal is the perfect way to relax after a hard day of hiking, and you don't have to know how to cook to eat like royalty. A variety of prepackaged envelopes of noodles complete with tasty sauces are now available from supermarkets everywhere. The same can be said of rice and potato dishes, which are available in box form; just add water and cook. Recipes for these packaged meals typically call for milk (which can be supplied in powdered form or omitted entirely) and butter (which is important; use squeezable margarine, which keeps forever). Complete freeze-dried meals are also available from backpacking specialty stores; they might be a feasible choice if you are independently wealthy. However, many freeze-dried foods have the same strong spices, and if used over a period of a week or more, they all begin to taste the same and may give you stomach problems.

A tin of kippered herrings or smoked oysters, or perhaps canned chicken, tuna, or salmon, rounds out the meal with enough protein to replace damaged muscle fibers. If you bring canned meat into the backcountry, be sure to wash out the can after use so that the odor of the meat does not attract unwanted campsite visitors, and pack out the tin. For vegetarians, hummus and falafel provide good alternatives to meat, in that they are rich in protein and come in a lightweight, powdered form that only requires water or a little oil for preparation.

Food Containers

When backpacking in Alaska, it is wise to bring a special container to hold your food and protect it from scavengers at night. Animals that succeed in getting food from campers lose their natural foraging habits and fear of humans. They then hang around human habitations, seeking scraps and garbage for their living. Such a habituated animal can be a nuisance if it is relatively small, like a ground squirrel. But if the interloper is a grizzly bear, it can turn into a deadly menace to that camper and to all humans that enter its home range later on. Ultimately, such a bear is likely to be shot as a "problem animal," even though the real problem lies with the people who allowed it to get into their food. Each backpacker who enters the Alaskan wilds is responsible for making absolutely certain that food and garbage are stowed in a way that makes them inaccessible to scavenging animals.

In Denali National Park, it is absolutely forbidden to embark on an overnight trip without carrying a bear-resistant food container ("bear bucket," for short) to protect your food. These cylinders are made from impact-resistant polymers, and have a large enough diameter to prevent even a large bear from getting its jaws around them. They are prone to warping if exposed to high temperatures, so keep them away from your stove. The bucket is opened by turning screws in the lid with a coin or pocketknife. The lid is flush with the body of the bucket, which prevents a bear from opening the bucket unless said bear happens to be carrying a screwdriver. Bear buckets can be leased or purchased in several locations around Alaska, usually for quite a steep price, and are available free of charge to backcountry visitors in Denali National Park.

If you cannot find or afford a bear bucket, you will need to hang your food out of reach of bears. A 20-liter drybag, of the type used by kayakers, makes a serviceable food bag. The thick rubber walls of the drybag are virtually airtight, and will slow the diffusion of scents to the outside environment. You will need about 30 feet of cord to hang your food (see Chapter 7 for details). Or if you are near a fairly deep body of water, you can tie your drybag to a stump and sink it below the surface of the water using a heavy boulder. The water flowing over the drybag virtually guarantees that an animal using smell to find its food will not be able to find yours.

When packing your food, you can save weight and space by repackaging dry items into sealable plastic baggies. Such baggies will mold themselves more efficiently into the limited space of your bearproof container or drybag. There are also tube-shaped containers on the market that have been designed specifically for backpacking. They work well for such liquid and paste items as peanut butter, honey, and margarine. As a reward for your repackaging efforts, you will have less garbage to pack out at the end of your trip. It makes sense to throw in an extra plastic bag expressly for carrying your garbage. Such bags are available free of charge at many ranger stations and visitor centers.

First Aid

Out in the backcountry, there aren't any first-aid stations to help you if you get injured. Carrying a small first-aid kit will help you handle most minor and major health problems that crop up during the course of your trip. Start out with a few Band-Aids, which are helpful for small cuts. For larger cuts, butterfly closures, which are X-shaped adhesive strips, will bind a wound together and slow bleeding. Sterile gauze bandages and first-aid tape are also basics for dealing with open cuts. A triangular bandage is particularly versatile. Bring along a small tin of Tylenol or ibuprofen. Not only do these drugs function as painkillers, but they also can reduce swelling in case of sprains. Ace bandages can provide further support for sprained joints. Don't forget some moleskin, because you will be using your feet hard, and blisters are a real possibility. Find out if members of your party have special health concerns, like asthma or allergies to bee stings, and make sure that the appropriate medications are not left behind. Finally, throw in a small tube of antibacterial cream so that you will have something to prevent wounds from getting infected.

Small Items

There are a few minor items that make life a whole lot easier. I like to bring a pair of cheap sunglasses for hiking in bright sunlight. These can save you from eyestrain and retinal damage on snowfields, glaciers, and at high altitudes. Look for sunglasses that give 100 percent protection from ultraviolet (UV) rays. If you have fair skin and anticipate traveling on snow, sunscreen will prove a valuable addition to your supplies. A good quality compass and the knowledge to use it will help you find your way in whiteouts and fog, when landmarks won't be there to guide you. And don't forget topographic maps of your area. Even if getting lost seems unlikely, topo maps will help you assess the exploratory potential of hidden landscapes. About 20 feet of light rope will help you cope with a variety of situations, foremost of which is hanging your pack beyond the reach of marauding animals.

Some hikers like to bring a flashlight with them into the woods. Dark nights are rarely a problem during the summer months, but even in the dark you will be better off without a flashlight. Flashlights narrow your field of vision to a small lighted circle, robbing you of peripheral vision. If you stand outside for a few minutes, your pupils will dilate and your eyes will become accustomed to the darkness. Thus attuned to your surroundings, you'll find that you trip over obstacles less frequently than when you are using a flashlight to light your way! In any case, hikers who visit Alaska will have difficulty finding a time when it is too dark to see.

The common pocketknife is about the most useful item you

can bring with you on your trip. Avoid ersatz survival gear such as the large Rambo-sized survival knives with hollow handles for fishhooks. These are too heavy and unwieldy even for butchering a moose, much less for carrying in a backpack as a utility tool. The Swiss-Army knives with a dozen blades provide a different kind of overkill; 80 percent of the blades may never see the light of day. A simple pocketknife with a curved cutting blade, a good can opener, and an awl will be sufficient for all of your backpacking needs. If your knife doesn't have a can opener, the US Army–style can opener weighs less than an ounce, fits on a key ring, and works quite well once you get the hang of it.

Loading Up for the Trip

Once you have assembled all of the gear you will need to complete your expedition, you must then decide which items you will want to have access to along the trail. Such items might include maps, snacks, a camera, your first-aid kit, warmer clothing, and raingear. These items should be placed in external pockets or in compartments where they can be accessed without unloading the entire pack. Items that will be used only when you reach camp can be buried in the depths of the pack. Inside the pack, your clothes should be sealed in plastic bags to prevent them from getting wet in case you fall while fording a stream.

When loading your gear, you must think about how to stow it in your pack so that the pack rides comfortably. Remember that the distribution of heavy objects within the pack determines the balance and comfort. For external-frame packs, the heaviest objects need to be closest to the top, resulting in a high center of gravity. Progressively lighter items should be distributed in the lower compartments and strapped securely to the frame below the packsack. For internal-frame packs, you want the center of gravity about midway up the pack and close to your back. Lighter gear should be placed above and below, and toward the outside of the pack. By placing the heaviest gear closest to your back, you will ensure that the pack remains stable on all kinds of terrain. In all cases, avoid tying heavy objects to the outside of your pack where they can swing around and upset your balance.

The weight of your pack will critically affect your enjoyment of the trip. A pack that is too heavy will exhaust you, and increase the likelihood of muscle pulls and other injuries. Men should carry an average of 40 pounds on their backs; this can be safely increased to 50 pounds for extended journeys. The average woman can handle a pack of 30 pounds without undue strain, and might increase the load to 35 pounds for longer trips. Most backpackers are fanatical about the weight of items that they pack, and will go to extremes to minimize weight. Some tricks to reduce weight include drilling holes in toothbrushes, bringing plastic picnic forks and spoons, and cutting towels in half to make them the minimum useful size. Remember, however, that it is unwise to compromise safety and other basic needs in the name of saving weight.

4 Maps and Navigation

PLANNING a backcountry expedition is as much a part of the wilderness experience as the hiking itself. An evening spent hovering over topographic maps, evaluating the ease and potential scenic value of various routes, is time well spent. By familiarizing yourself with the lay of the country *before* you actually get there, you accord yourself the advantage of preparedness in dealing with challenging terrain. Staring into maps, the mind's eye transforms lines into ranges, passes, and valleys, and difficult crossings are negotiated mentally long before they are attempted on foot. Cultivating a love for maps will increase your appreciation for the sweep of country that lies ahead, and will give you a headstart in navigating the wilds successfully.

In clear weather, it is easy to pick out landmarks along your route and chart your course through mountainous terrain. Mountain weather is frequently uncooperative, however, and you may be lucky to see only the bases of the peaks arrayed about you. In snowstorms and fog, visibility may be cut even further to a few hundred feet ahead, and you will be completely reliant on map and compass to navigate through the murk. In the flat, featureless terrain of much of the forested interior you will find no landmarks to help you navigate. Hence, it is necessary to become familiar with the workings of compass and map so that together they can aid you when the need arises.

Reading a Topo Map

Topographic (or topo) maps are your key to the secrets of the mountains. These maps, which are generally quite accurate, are invaluable for selecting a passable route through difficult terrain. When planning your trip, purchase the map sheets, called *quadrangles,* which correspond to the area you intend to explore. If these maps are not available locally, they can be ordered by mail from the office of the US Geological Survey and its Canadian counterpart, at the addresses in "The Explorer's Directory" at the back of the book. Spend at least half an hour poring over the maps, evaluating various routes for their potential scenic value and ease of passage. Topo maps are chock-full of useful information, and it is well worth taking the time to learn the ins and outs of interpreting them.

Topo maps are no substitute for the detailed information that can be gathered from local sources, however. Many of these maps were drawn decades ago, and river channels and glaciers may no longer be accurately represented. River depths are not represented, and a stream that appears small on a map may in fact be swift and deep. In addition, some of these maps have 100-foot contours. These large-scale contour lines may not show the small-scale obstacles, like low bands of cliff, that might impede cross-country travel. Be sure to talk to land managers or local residents to fill in the information gaps left by topographic maps.

Understanding Contour Lines

Contour lines are used to display elevation and relief on topo maps. By interpreting contour lines, you can visualize peaks and valleys, passes and cliffs, and other features of the physical landscape. These lines are the basic code of all topo maps, so it is imperative to have a solid understanding of how to interpret them.

Imagine for a moment a classic three-layered wedding cake. Perhaps the first layer is 1 foot high, the second layer 2 feet above the base, and the third layer reaches 3 feet; each layer has a larger diameter than the one above. If the baker iced a green trim around the top edge of each layer, then the green icing could be used as contour lines. If you viewed the cake from above, you would see three nested circles of green icing, each one corresponding to an altitude above the base of the cake. Each of the green circles follows one elevation precisely, neither rising above its level nor dipping below the surface of the layer. These circles of frosting could be labeled "1 foot," "2 feet," and "3 feet," allowing the baker to draw a plan of the wedding cake on a two-dimensional sheet of paper. An assistant could then use the plan to produce a real cake. If a scale was included, the assistant would know exactly how large in diameter each layer was supposed to be.

Now imagine a cake in the shape of a cone. The same baker could apply frosting in a circle around the cone at varying elevations above the base, with elevation labels on each one. An assistant viewing it from the top would know how wide the cone was at each elevation. However, the assistant would *not* know whether the elevations ascended in a steplike pattern like the classic wedding cake or smoothly like a cone. The two-dimensional plan gives no information about the shape of the cake between the contour lines. Therefore, the plan for the cone-shaped cake might look identical to the plan for the three-layered wedding cake!

The previous examples illustrate the basic concept of how contour lines work. Their shortcoming is that they tell nothing about the area between the lines. However, in the case of topo maps, the lines are typically so close together that the area between them is quite small, and it is useful to assume that a smooth, unbroken plane connects the contour lines. Of course, the surface of a mountain landscape is infinitely more complex than a simple layered cake or cone. Fortunately, however, topo maps slice the mountains horizontally at regular intervals, from top to bottom, revealing the complexities of the mountains' three-dimensional relief. And they do all this on a flat piece of paper that you can carry with you easily.

Map series A illustrates this principle in detail. First, take a look at the photograph at the top of page 75. This is the landscape as you would view it from the ground. The sketch at the bottom of page 74 shows the same landscape, with contour

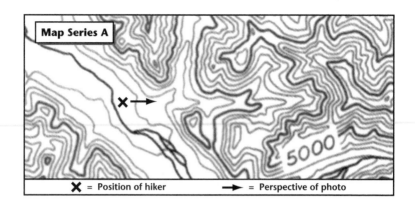

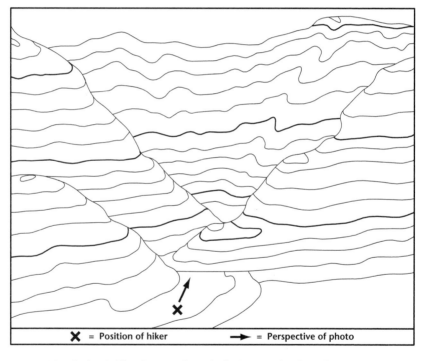

Map Series A: The photograph on the facing page has been diagrammed here in three dimensions with contour lines. Compare the photo and diagram with the corresponding topographic map above.

lines superimposed at regular height intervals onto the surface of the land. At the top of page 74 is the topo map corresponding to this landscape as it would look if viewed from an airplane flying over the site. Notice that the overhead view provided by the topo map provides a lot of information about parts of the landscape that are hidden from the observer.

Once you get accustomed to thinking in contour lines, you can begin using this skill to interpret landscapes without actually seeing them. This is the beauty and usefulness of topo maps. Because contour lines are always drawn at a constant elevation, they will tell you how steep the terrain is. Contour lines that are very close together describe terrain that has considerable vertical rise per unit of horizontal distance. Cliffs are the most extreme example of this principle (see map series B on page 76), and are displayed by a series of nearly touching contour lines. At the other end of the spectrum, contour lines spaced widely apart denote relatively flat areas like valley floors and benches.

As you look at topo maps, you will notice that some con-

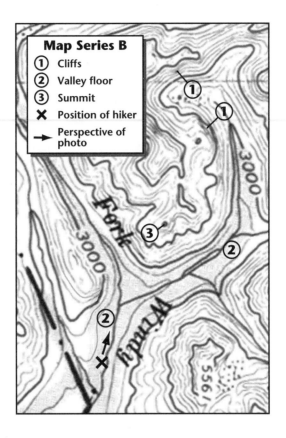

tour lines form closed loops and some do not. Closed loops describe features that stick up vertically from the surrounding landscape. In low-lying areas such as valleys, hillsides may grade into each other in a long series rather than rising independently from the valley floor. You can use this distinction to identify mountaintops, which rise independently and thus are expressed as loops on topo maps.

It is useful to start with the watercourses when examining a topo map. Watercourses will always be at the lowest part of a valley or ravine, because water always flows downhill. Once you have identified a stream flowing through the bottom of a valley by its thin blue line, you can follow it up its gradient to the source, which will be shown simply as the end of the stream

Map Series B: A traveler standing at spot "x" and looking up Windy Creek could determine the pattern of cliffs and valleys that lie ahead from the topographic map, shown on the facing page.

line on the map. You can be sure that you are tracing the watercourse upstream by using the contour lines that it crosses as guides. Where a stream crosses a contour line, the contour line will almost always be bent in a concave shape. Think of a stream crossing through the letter *C* from left to right. The front of the *C*, with the opening, will face downstream while the rounded back of the *C* points uphill. Once you have identified the valley floor and the direction of water flow using this method, you can allow your eyes to wander outward toward the walls of the valley.

Take a look at the valley bottom in map series C (pages 78-79). From the perspective of the hiker, you can follow the river upstream, across broad flats and up through a narrow gap in the hills to the glacial valley beyond. What you can't see from the photo is that at the head of the valley, the river separates into three distinct branches, each with its own smaller valley that joins with the others where the streams converge. Narrow, fingerlike contour lines project into the valley from each side; these represent the ridgelines that rise from the valley floor to the summits of surrounding hills, providing passable routes for hikers on their way to the summits. The value of topo maps in seeing the country beyond the horizon is apparent in this exercise.

Elevations. Topographic maps work on the principle that smaller things are stacked on top of larger things in a continuous chain. Therefore, concentric contour lines stacked one inside the other denote a gain in elevation up to a small summit. Elevations are marked along thick contour lines at regular intervals. Marked elevations are expressed as distance above sea level, and thus mountains that are not considered lofty on the basis of their summit elevation can be quite imposing if their base is at a low elevation. On most maps, every fifth line is a thick contour line, and these thick lines are separated in most

Map Series C: The branching valleys at the head of the Savage River cannot be seen in this photo, but show up clearly on the topographic map (opposite).

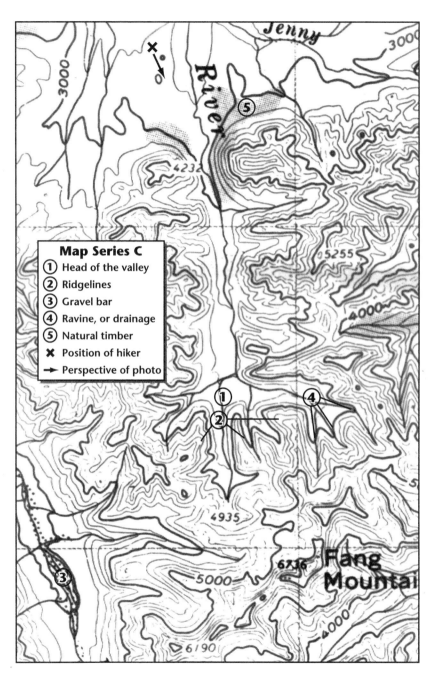

Map Series C
① Head of the valley
② Ridgelines
③ Gravel bar
④ Ravine, or drainage
⑤ Natural timber
✖ Position of hiker
➡ Perspective of photo

cases by a vertical distance of 500 feet. The distance between the thinner lines can be deduced by dividing the overall distance between the thick lines by the number of line intervals (not thin lines) between the thick lines. In many cases, there are five intervals between thick contours, and thus each fine contour line represents an elevation gain of 100 feet. Exact elevations of summits and passes are frequently marked in addition to contour lines, and provide useful points of reference. The elevation of the surface of large lakes is marked in blue on the lake's surface, providing another reference elevation for hikers. The depth of lakes is not marked on topo maps.

For older map series in the United States and Canada, elevations are expressed in feet. However, the newer map series is changing over to metric measurements, and elevations are expressed in meters. There are 3.28 feet to a meter, so if you don't think in metric you can multiply metric elevations by three to yield the approximate elevation in feet.

Depressions. Because the overhead view of depression contours would look exactly like the contours of a hill, mappers use a special contour line with tiny hatch marks pointing downhill to denote depressions. When you see concentric circles of this type of contour line, you are looking at a basin with no drainage outlet.

Passes. Between mountaintops are saddles where you can often make a passage between neighboring valleys. These saddles are denoted on topo maps by two closed loops that approach each other, but do not quite touch (see map series D on pages 82-83). The distance between the contour lines where the loops converge describes the width of the pass itself. Broad passes are expressed by contour lines that are far apart where the loops come near one another, while steep-sided notches between the peaks are denoted by contour lines that are close together in the vicinity of the saddle. When assessing the breadth of a pass, you should draw an imaginary line along the spine of the ridges above each side of the pass. You can evaluate how far apart the contour lines are as they pass through this imaginary line to get a better feeling for the true slope of the ridgelines as they converge at the pass.

Your ability to traverse a given pass is not determined by the breadth of the pass, but by the steepness of the slopes leading up to it. To evaluate a pass for travel, take a look at the steepness of the valley's head where it approaches the pass. Many valleys, especially those of glacial origin, will terminate in a headwall of steep cliffs that is completely impassable to all but wild sheep and goats. Other valleys may rise steadily to a pass, requiring a hard slog up meadow slopes to reach the next drainage. Other passes—those formed by large glaciers that slopped over into several distinct drainages—tend to be long and narrow with gentle slopes, and are ideal for moving between major drainages.

Water

Water is shown in light blue on topo maps, but the names of bodies of water are often written in black. On quadrangles that are provisional (not yet completed), water will appear in black, with a crosshatched surface. Still and moving water are not specifically differentiated on maps, but you can infer that bodies of water that cross contour lines are indeed streams and not lakes. Inlets and outlets of lakes are also not differentiated, but the direction of water flow can be determined by looking at the elevations of the contour lines that the stream crosses. Some lakes have a number printed on them, which is the elevation of the lake's surface above sea level (not its depth).

The swiftness of a stream can be deduced by the slope of the streambed, as indicated by the number of contour lines (representing vertical elevation) that a stream crosses in a given distance. Rapids are rarely indicated on topo maps, but frequently occur where a watercourse reaches a steeper downhill section of its valley. Waterfalls are indicated by short blue lines across the stream at right angles to its direction of flow. Meandering streambeds that loop back on themselves fre-

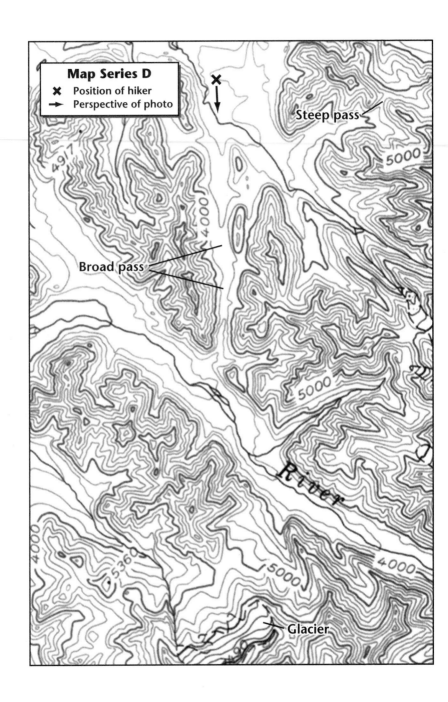

Map Series D: This gap corresponds to the broad pass on the map on the facing page; the glaciated peak rises beyond the river.

quently are generally slow moving and potentially deep.

In Alaska, many rivers flow over beds of unstable gravel. These gravels are continually being pushed around by the changing flow of the watercourse, forming temporary dams that cause the waters to seek new passages. As the water continually seeks the lowest passage through the gravel, the channel may split into many smaller streams called *braids*. Topo maps show all stream channels, not just the main one, and thus it is possible to find stream braids easily for the purpose of fording a stream. However, these channels change frequently over the course of time, and topo maps typically do not reflect the current position of these channels. If the stream runs across a barren gravel bar, the bar will be indicated on the map by a cluster of fine brown dots covering the extent of the barren area. Intermittent streams, which dry up during some part of the summer, are indicated by a blue line separated by a couple of broken dashes at regular intervals. Such streams can generally be counted on to carry water following rainstorms, and also during spring runoff.

Other Features

The boundaries of glaciers and permanent snowfields are indicated on topo maps by regular dashed blue lines. Contour lines on glaciers and snowfields will be marked in blue rather than brown. If the glacier is covered in debris, the boundaries and contours will be marked in blue, while the surface of the glacier will be covered with small brown dots much like a gravel bar. In some of the larger icefields, crevasses are marked by short, solid blue lines.

Glaciers provide a good example of the limitations of the 100-foot contour interval. What appears to be a gently sloping flat of ice may really be a rugged moonscape of moraines, ice ridges, and caves that are too small to show up on the map. In addition, the glacier may have surged or retreated since the map was drawn.

A few vegetation features are commonly denoted on topo maps. Harvestable timber, defined as the presence of any commercially used tree species at any stage of development, is marked by light green shading on the brown contour lines of the physical landscape. In Alaska, this usually means spruce of some variety, and excludes tall brush that can be a real hindrance to travel. Note the shaded areas at the mouth of the canyon in map series C (pages 78-79) that indicate the spruce stands visible in the photograph. Because there are no shaded regions on the map farther up the valley, you can conclude that there are no spruce trees in the headwaters, even though you cannot see the upper reaches of the valley in the photograph. Marshes and boggy areas are often indicated by special symbols that look like clumps of grass with a line below them.

Constructed or artificial features are also clearly shown by topo maps. Maintained roads of varying grade are shown as unbroken parallel lines in black ink. Jeep trails, accessible only to four-wheel-drive vehicles during good weather, appear as paired dashed lines. Single dashed lines indicate the presence of developed horse and foot trails. You should check locally to find out if these trails are still being maintained. Small black squares indicate cabins and other structures, which may or may not be in a good state of repair. A crossed pick and shovel symbol indicates the presence of a mine site. Mine sites are dangerous in that they are often riddled with unstable tunnels into which the unwary hiker can fall. It is best to avoid them altogether.

Map and Compass Skills

The compass was developed during the Renaissance to aid mariners in navigating across featureless seas. It is just as useful today in helping backpackers navigate through unfamiliar territory. The basic compass consists of a magnetized needle set in a liquid medium above a card with the degrees of a circle marked on it. One end of the needle is impregnated with magnetite, which is attracted to the North Magnetic Pole of the earth.

Magnetic Versus Geographic North

The North Magnetic Pole does not coincide exactly with the true North Pole of the earth. Rather, the North Magnetic Pole currently lies in northern Canada, far to the south of the geographic pole. In Alaska, your compass will point to a spot that is considerably east of true North, and you must compensate for this by adjusting your compass bearings a number of degrees to the west in order to reflect the true directions. The degree of error between true North and magnetic North is known as the *declination* (see Figure 1). A typical declination (taken from Wrangell–St. Elias National Park) of 29 degrees illustrates the importance of accounting for this phenomenon when navigating by compass. A hiking party that erroneously used the unmodified true North bearing on the map to orient themselves would, after a distance of only 3 miles, estimate their position to be 1.5 miles east of their true location on the landscape!

Fortunately, the US Geologic Survey includes a compass declination on each of its topo maps to help you orient your map and compass correctly. The declination diagram is specific to the area covered by the map, and varies considerably from region to region. On maps showing large areas, the declination may even change from one side of the map to the other. The diagram consists of two arrows joined at their bases, with the angle of declination printed between the arrows. The right-hand arrow signifies the direction of magnetic North (to which your compass will point), while the left-hand arrow points to the geographic pole.

The angle of declination is the number of compass degrees of adjustment that should be made in order to correct compass bearings to reflect true geographic directions. Some compasses have an arrow that moves independently of the dial to correct for the declination. If this is the case, you can simply set the arrow at the proper number of degrees east of North that is indicated on your topo map. The needle can then simply be centered on this arrow, which now points to magnetic North, and readings taken from the dial will reflect true geographic directions. If your compass lacks this feature, you can still carefully center the needle on the indicated number of degrees east of North to take proper bearings on the landscape.

Using a Compass to Navigate

Cross-country navigation begins at the trailhead. When you first get out of your vehicle, take the time to look at your topo map and compare it to the landscape. Note any prominent features that lie along your intended route of travel; you will use them as landmarks as you go. This activity, known as getting your bearings, will prepare you for successful navigation by forcing you to contemplate the relationships among your car, your objective, and intermediate landscape features or obstacles. Without this initial frame of reference, your compass and map will be of very little help.

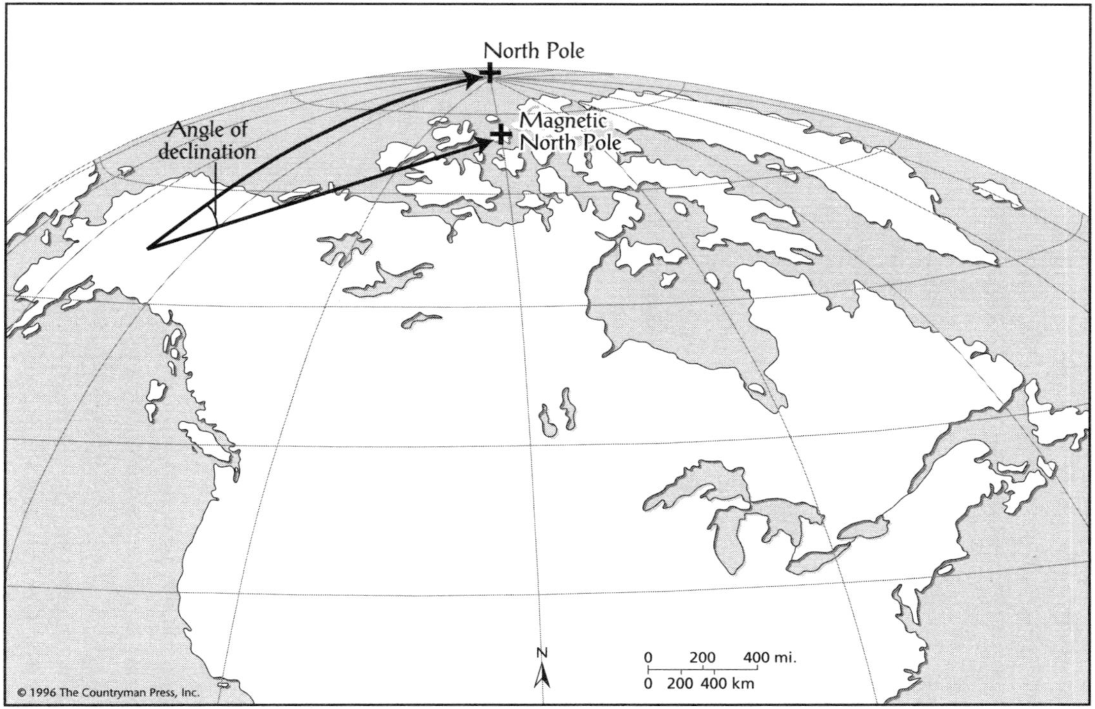

FIGURE 1. *Since your compass needle is drawn to the magnetic North Pole and not the geographic North Pole (or true north), you need to compensate for this degree of error, or angle of declination, to chart an accurate course on your map. Specific information is given on USGS maps, and varies from region to region.*

Establishing a Baseline. Roads, streams, power lines, and pipelines all cross the landscape in a continuous line, and make useful baselines for navigation. This very basic form of route-finding is useful if you need to find your way back to a known point along the baseline. It works well even when it is foggy or there are no visible terrain features.

The use of baselines for navigation assumes that you know approximately where you are in relation to the baseline. Because a compass needle always points to magnetic North, you can always determine your approximate direction of travel simply by referring frequently to your compass. Try to hike away from the baseline along a single compass bearing, without deviating far from that straight line. When you are ready to return, orient your compass properly and extend the bearing backward through the dial of the compass 180 degrees. This will give you the most direct bearing for your return. There is one disadvantage, however: You will emerge on the baseline near your starting point, but will not know whether to turn left or right to reach it. It is better to choose a return bearing that is 5 degrees to one side of the most direct route. With this built-in error, you will know which way to go when you emerge on the baseline.

To fully grasp this concept, imagine that some backpackers have hiked due east from a highway to reach a distant lake. They will need to orient their compass and take a westward bearing to return to the car. However, since the highway is long, linear, and featureless, they should alter their angle of return from the original path. In this example, our hikers will take an angle slightly south of west when returning. That way, when they strike the road, they will know that the car lies to the north, and they need to turn right to reach it.

Triangulation: Pinpointing Your Position. You can also use a compass and map to find your exact position in the landscape (see Figure 2). First, orient the map so that the compass needle and the magnetic North arrow on the map are pointing in exactly the same direction. By doing this, you can be certain the bearings to known landmarks are the same on the map and on the physical landscape. Next, line up a known object on the landscape such as a mountaintop or small lake with the center pin of your compass, and read the number of degrees from magnetic North. Next, set the compass on the map and draw a line through the landmark at the exact angle from magnetic North that was indicated by your compass when you took your sighting of the landmark. Repeat this process for a second known landmark that is marked on your map, drawing a line at the appropriate angle through this second feature. Finally, extend the two lines that you have drawn until they cross, and this intersection will mark your exact position on the map. This method of direction finding is called triangulation.

Charting a Straight-line Course. Once you have determined your position on the map, you can then use the compass to indicate the direction that you must travel in order to reach a destination that is beyond your line of sight. This time, put the compass down on the map, lined up with magnetic North, and take a sighting on the *map,* determining the number of degrees between magnetic North and the invisible line running through your destination point. Then remove the compass from the map, and with the needle still pointing at o degrees, line up the center post of the compass and the number of degrees from zero that you measured from your map. This sighting will indicate the direction of travel you must take to reach your destination in a straight line.

You may encounter obstacles during the course of navigation that will cause you to deviate from a straight-line compass bearing. One solution to this problem is to sight on a series of landmarks that lie beyond the obstacle along the compass bearing. You can then depart from the bearing to negotiate the obstacle, and then return to your original path by lining up the chosen landmarks.

If no such landmarks make themselves apparent, you can make a compass detour around the obstacle. To do so, turn 90 degrees away from the compass bearing, and begin counting the number of steps you take. As soon as possible, return to a

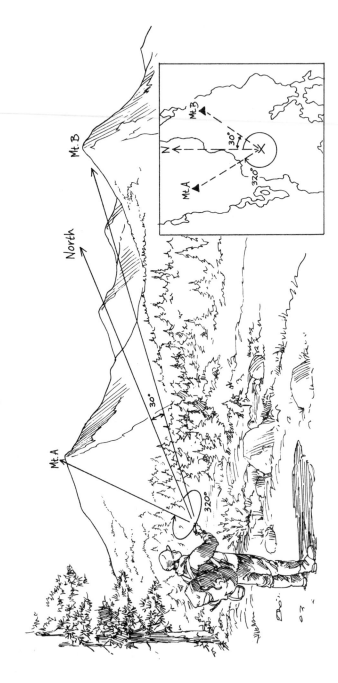

FIGURE 2. To pinpoint where you are on your map, you can use a technique called triangulation. This hiker has taken bearings on two mountaintops that are easily identified on the map. A bearing on Mt. A reads 320 degrees, and a bearing on Mt. B reads 30 degrees. The hiker is standing approximately where the two bearings intersect on the map.

course parallel to the original compass bearing. Finally, with the obstacle behind you, take another 90-degree turn back toward the original bearing, and follow this course for the same number of steps that you took to get around the obstacle. After covering this distance, you can return to the original compass bearing, and will have returned to your original heading with very little deviation.

Pitfalls and Proper Use. Your ability to navigate by using a compass depends on the accuracy of the compass bearings that you take. An error of only 2 or 3 degrees can amount to a sizable difference in your position after only a few miles. If you are relying on your compass alone to navigate, be a stickler for accuracy and take your time to do it right. It is most desirable to use terrain features on a map to continuously correct your estimated position. By taking compass bearings frequently, errors will be erased as new sightings are made, and you can more easily prevent yourself from becoming lost. Take bearings on intermediate features such as rock outcrops or distinctive trees, and use them as goals. This will allow you to remain on course in a landscape that rarely allows easy straight-line travel.

Under certain circumstances, a compass may give you a misleading bearing. These situations can be avoided by learning the proper way to hold your compass and by being aware of problem objects in your immediate vicinity. To be certain that your readings are not affected by gravity, you must hold the compass as close to level as possible. Be aware that magnetized metal objects and electrical sources can cause a compass to give you misleading information. Hold the compass away from your body so that keys or zippers do not interfere with the direction of the compass needle. Do not trust bearings that are taken close to electric power lines or stations, and avoid the use of small electrical devices (including flashlights) near the compass while you are taking your bearings.

Global Positioning Systems

For hikers who have a true fear of getting lost, hand-held Global Positioning System (GPS) units are a new option. These units use a network of orbiting satellites to triangulate an exact position on the ground. Most GPS units give latitude and longitude coordinates, which also appear on your topographic maps. Remember that each degree of latitude is broken into 60 minutes that are counted from south to north, and each degree of longitude is broken into 60 minutes that are counted from east to west. GPS units can't navigate for you; once you have plotted your position, you will still need a map and compass to plan your course. Many purists consider GPS units to be at odds with wilderness travel traditions. They are also quite expensive. Nonetheless, a GPS unit can be a valuable form of insurance for backpackers seeking an extra line of defense against getting lost.

Celestial Navigation Aids

The sun and stars have been used for navigation throughout human history. In Alaska, these celestial objects are much less reliable as navigation tools. The far northern latitudes of the 49th state confuse the traditional east-west track of the sun. During the height of summer, the sun may rise high in the northeast, then roll around to the south as it ascends during the height of the day. The sun continues to track to the west and north after midday, and may finally set in the northwest in the evening. At higher latitudes, the sun never sets during the evening, but merely rolls around the northern horizon, confusing the issue even further. The opposite trend occurs during winter, when the sun may clear the southern horizon for a few hours if the weather cooperates.

Alaskan summer nights feature daylight practically around the clock, and the stars cannot be counted on during early- and midsummer, when the sky never gets dark enough to render them visible. However, when the night sky is visible, the North

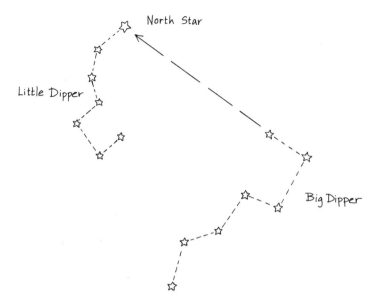

FIGURE 3. *The two stars at the edge of the Big Dipper line up with the North Star.*

Star provides a useful navigation aid. The North Star occupies a constant position above the North Geographic Pole, and thus provides an unerring reference point for travelers. Some topo maps even signify true geographic North by a star on the compass declination diagram in deference to the usefulness of the North Star as a navigation aid.

The North Star is the endmost star in the handle of the Little Dipper constellation, which is shaped like a cooking pot. The easiest way to find it is to look for the brighter and more prominent Big Dipper, which occupies a position in the northern sky. The two stars at the front of the Big Dipper's "pot" line up to point directly at the North Star, as can be seen in Figure 3. If you happen to forget this handy arrangement, you can remind yourself by looking at the Alaska state flag, which portrays the Big Dipper and the North Star against a field of blue.

On Getting Lost

Backpacking in Alaska demands a high level of self-sufficiency. In the more remote parts of the state, no one will happen along to help you out if you get into trouble. If you become disoriented in the Alaskan backcountry, your ability to return to civilization depends on your preparedness and ability to navigate.

The first step in preventing a disaster is to notify a few responsible folks where you are going and how long you will be gone. Have them send out a search party if you are overdue for more than 2 days. Some government agencies will allow you to check in before and after your trip; if you take advantage of this service, *be absolutely sure* that you do not fail to return and report in when you get back.

If you fail to report your trip to someone you can trust, you may never be missed. A man was found dead just north of Denali National Park in the summer of 1992. He had kept a diary of his ordeal. It records how he injured himself falling through the ice of a frozen stream, and afterward hunkered down in an abandoned school bus to wait for help. He survived for 2 months, but no one came along in time to save him. Ultimately, he succumbed to starvation. If you leave an itinerary with someone before you leave, your absence will be noticed and a search-and-rescue party will know where to start looking.

Provided someone knows where you are headed, the best bet if you get lost is to move to a highly visible place and stay put. Several years ago, a couple of off-duty rangers at Denali National Park embarked on an ill-advised ascent of Scott Peak during a stormy fall weekend. They became lost after summitting, and came down the mountain on the wrong side of the Alaska Range. Search parties were organized when they failed to return, and after 5 days they were finally found, somewhat thinner but none the worse for wear. If they had tried to walk out, given their disorientation, they never would have made it back. By staying in one spot, the rangers maximized their chances of rescue, because they remained closer to the area in which the search was focused rather than moving away from it.

If you are lost and awaiting a search party, your prime directive is to find an open place and make yourself as visible as possible. An example from my own past dramatizes this point. Several years ago, I took part in a ground-based search for a missing hiker in Denali National Park. An aerial search had been combing the area for the previous 3 days, but was unable to locate the missing hiker's tent and camp, which we found later in a stand of sparse spruce trees. Your visibility to an aircraft overhead is hampered by your relatively small size and the pilot's possible preoccupation with the complexities of flying. There are several ways to advertise your presence to overflying aircraft and to communicate your distress to the pilot.

You should make your distress signals as obvious as possible. Flare guns offer one effective way to signal distress, but these are rarely carried into the backcountry by hikers because of their weight and bulk. If you are hunting, three shots fired in even succession signify distress to a trained ear. Three dots, three dashes, and three dots signify Morse code for "SOS," the universal distress signal. The code can be flashed with a mirror or other reflective item, or by using a flashlight at night. Be aware, however, that most ordinary folk are not clued in to this sort of communication, and may fail to correctly interpret your distress signal. Fires are good signals as well, and should be made bright at night and smoky during the daytime for best visibility. Finally, if none of these tools is available to you, you can spread out bright-colored clothing on the open ground to try to attract the attention of overflying aircraft.

By far, however, the best hedge against being lost is prevention through preparedness. Always try to keep track of your position in relation to prominent landmarks in the environment. Visualize in your mind what the landscape ahead should look like, and compare what you see in the bush to the markings on your topo maps. Finally, do not panic under any circumstances, because a cool wit is always better at finding solutions to the most perplexing situations.

5 Route Selection

$\mathbf{I}$N Alaska and the Yukon, most
of the wilderness areas—even in the national parks—lack developed trails. If you want to see the wonders of the land beyond
the highway, you must be versed in the skills of cross-country
travel. This means reading the landscape as a whole, and evaluating the infinite array of route choices to find the right one for
you. This process is more art than science, and you will find
that by leaving the trail behind, you will participate more completely in the surrounding landscape. Each footstep will require you to think about the terrain you are passing over, and
you will leave with a much more vivid recollection of the
Alaskan wilderness than can be gained by any other means.

A Few Words on Cross-Country Hiking

Off-trail hiking requires an entirely new set of skills. Uneven
surfaces are the rule, and obstacles such as fallen trees, rocks,
and roots must be negotiated. In the absence of a designated
travel route, you will need to select a path through the landscape that requires minimal effort and avoids safety hazards.
This section will first discuss the techniques of cross-country
walking as they differ from hiking on trails; the more complex
task of route selection will be tackled in following sections of
this chapter.

Walking would seem to be a natural skill; after all, we have all
been doing it since we were toddlers. However, walking cross-
country requires entirely different muscles and a new level of

awareness of foot placement than does walking on an even surface. The first rule of thumb in cross-country travel is to slow down. You will need to learn to choose the placement of each footstep with care, in order to avoid entanglements or potholes. After a time, you will develop a comfortable rhythm of walking that eats up the miles with minimal effort. Hikers new to cross-country travel typically push the pace to equal their travel rates on trails. This is generally a mistake, because such hikers tire quickly and require frequent rest stops. It is much more efficient to travel at a slow but sustainable pace. A slower pace will also improve your ability to avoid obstacles that might cause you injury.

The most efficient way to deal with obstacles in your path is to avoid them entirely. Our culture extols the virtue of a straight-line approach, but this philosophy is counterproductive when applied to off-trail hiking. It takes much more energy to surmount an obstacle than it does to go around. In addition, you will find it necessary to break your walking rhythm in order to negotiate such an obstacle, and this will slow your journey significantly when compared with a simple detour. Finally, climbing under or over objects in your path of travel may increase the danger of an accident or injury that would ruin the whole trip.

There will be times when the tundra seems interminable, when each step seems to bring you no closer to your destination. When you or one of your party falls into this kind of slump, it helps to have a concrete method for convincing yourself and others to make tracks when it seems futile to do so. Here are a few things you can do to help the miles slide by more easily when each foot seems to weigh a ton.

First of all, you can set small goals. Look into the intermediate distance and identify a topographic feature such as the next stream course or an oddly shaped hill. Establish this feature as a short-range goal for yourself, and focus on it rather than the larger goal of your ultimate destination. When you reach this goal, you will have a small feeling of accomplishment (or relief) that will fuel your desire to go farther. In addition, by reaching an intermediate goal, you will prove to your dubious mind that you are actually making progress. When you feel like you are accomplishing something, the whole process of backpacking becomes much more enjoyable.

Secondly, reward yourself from time to time as you reach set goals. I like to postpone my lunch break until I have negotiated a difficult obstacle such as a river crossing or a mountain pass. Smaller rewards, such as a snack or a water break, can be used as incentives to reach intermediate-range goals. Discipline yourself to use rest stops as rewards for goals, and remember that if you take a lot of rest stops, your ground speed will decrease in spectacular fashion. Resist the temptation to rest every few hundred yards when tired; it is much better to have one long rest stop to recuperate and then have a long, productive period of hiking.

If individuals in your party are lagging behind, you will need to buoy their flagging spirits and instill in them the discipline needed to reach your destination. Avoid criticism in times like these, because those who are mentally defeated will only sink deeper into self-pity if you use this tack. Instead, give them encouragement, and show them evidence that the miles are indeed passing. Wait for them if they fall behind, because they will be able to hike faster if they have the illusion that they might be able to keep up with the other members of the party. Be certain that they have plenty of water, because dehydration only accelerates exhaustion. When you reach your destination, congratulate your partners on their grit, and give the weaker ones a breather while you prepare lunch or set up camp.

The Path of Least Resistance

Consider, for a moment, a wolf running through the forest. It moves with grace and ease, picking out a safe and rapid route through the underbrush. The wolf neither slows its pace nor crashes through noisily, but glides swiftly and silently, like an apparition. Wild animals instinctively follow the path of least resistance, taking a more circuitous route that requires less time and effort than a more direct path. They are intimately in tune with their environments. Most animals occupy well-defined home ranges in which they spend their entire lives. As a result of years and years of recrossing the same terrain, the animal becomes intimately familiar with its habitat. The short Alaskan growing season provides animals a limited window of opportunity to lay on reserves of fat for the long, cold winter. Consequently, animals must always use the most efficient routes for their travels, because to do otherwise draws down their energy reserves and uses valuable time that could have been spent foraging for food. As a result, they follow paths of least resistance between foraging and resting sites, and their activities leave well-defined game trails that crisscross the landscape.

Human society, by contrast, conditions us to believe that the shortest distance between two points is a straight line. But in the wilderness, you will rarely be afforded a straight, easy path that leads directly to your destination. Thus, you can either bull your way through a clump of brush or straight over every hill and hummock, or follow the natural roll of the topography and vegetation—which will afford you easier hiking and will often get you there more quickly as well.

You can take advantage of the instinctive tendency of wild animals to seek the path of least resistance by following their trails. Remember that each animal has its own agenda, and it will rarely correspond exactly to your goal of traveling long distances. On the contrary, game trails typically connect feeding sites along corridors of easy travel, such as ridgelines and stream banks. Smaller trails may run laterally across hillsides, connecting patches of favorable vegetation. In all cases, you will constantly need to evaluate the game trail to see if you might be better off getting onto another one. The best strategy is to follow a game trail until it starts taking you away from your destination; then switch to a different trail.

Game trails provide especially good travel corridors for a number of reasons. First of all, the passage of hoofed animals packs down the soil, making a firm walking surface. Regular use by animals also tends to break off branches and roots lying across the path that might otherwise catch your foot and send you for a header. Wild herbivores are even more fearful of bears than you are, and will tend to travel in places where they cannot easily be ambushed. As herbivores move along, they constantly sample the vegetation around them. Over many years, this browsing clears the area immediately next to the trail, providing better visibility. As a result, game trails are often as good or better than designated hiking trails, because their constant use provides "maintenance" on a regular basis that cannot be matched by any land management agency.

If you have a hard time finding game trails, you can still use the path of least resistance to make your travels easier and more enjoyable. The key to this strategy is to evaluate the mosaic of habitat types beforehand and then select a route that connects the most favorable ones. The choice is usually fairly apparent: climbing onto a well-drained hillside to avoid brush fields or tussocks, or wading up a streambed to avoid the ups and downs of broken terrain. Remember that you can spend an hour fighting your way through half a mile of dense brush or tussock tundra, so a detour to firmer ground, even if it doubles the distance you have to travel or the altitude you must gain, may well be worth the extra effort. In general, you should seek routes characterized by firm footing, sparse vegetation, and flat relief.

When hiking uphill, you can also take a lesson from the wild inhabitants of the bush. Animals rarely walk straight uphill; rather, they pick a more gentle angle of ascent that allows them to walk continuously without pausing to regain their breath. You will find that hill climbing is much easier if you do the same, following imaginary switchbacks that trade off steepness for distance. The same idea applies to descents. The foot-pounding impacts of downhill travel are jarring to the knees and ankles, and the excess speed of rapid descent goes hand in hand with the carelessness that leads to injury. By zigzagging across a slope, you can bleed off some of your foot speed and enjoy a more controlled descent.

Ridge Running

Ridgelines provide direct access to the higher ground, and can often be followed for miles. These are strenuous travel routes, and often require steep, calf-burning ascents and lots of ups and downs. Despite these disadvantages, ridgelines commonly sport major game trails, and should be considered as a possible alternative to valley travel where the country is not too steep. Ridgelines occur at the boundaries of watersheds, and thus are well drained and provide good footing. They also afford spectacular views in places where the vegetation is not too tall. Once you clear the treeline, the brush falls away and is replaced by alpine tundra, which provides some of the easiest walking around. However, this same tundra can be quite fragile, especially on semi-arid sites. Watch for lichens and bare ground, which indicate especially delicate sites, and avoid walking there.

When evaluating a ridgeline as a travel option, safety should be your first concern. Although the very spine of the ridge often affords level footing (even when both sides fall away into sheer cliffs), steep terrain should be avoided at all costs. If the spine of the ridge starts to break up into sheer faces, it probably won't be long before you are forced to backtrack and find another route anyway, so it is best to avoid this situation entirely by descending onto more gentle terrain when the going starts to get hairy on top. Remember that rocky footing is not always stable, especially if it is loose or made of crumbly material.

Streams as Travel Corridors

Streambeds are often the safest, most convenient, and easiest access routes into the high country. They are veritable highways for wildlife, and as a result tend to be well endowed with game trails. However, streamside vegetation tends to be lush, and impenetrable brush is not uncommon at low elevations. Fording the stream may be necessary at frequent intervals. But because water always seeks the lowest point, traveling up streambeds will not entail unnecessary ups and downs, and I haven't yet heard of anyone falling to his death from a stream bank. Here are some pointers to help you decide if streambeds are the right way to get around where you are going.

Gravel bars are one of the favorite travel corridors of seasoned backpackers in Alaska. When Alaskans speak of gravel bars, they are not talking about piles of gravel in a river, they are talking about broad outwash plains covered entirely in cobbles, with a braided stream running down the center. The gravel bar is maintained by the constant shifting of the stream's course in the valley. The constant downward flow of rocks and boulders dams up the stream in one place, but because the gravel is unstable throughout the valley, the stream is able to find another course, and thus the open nature of the bar is maintained. The water level is rarely high enough to cover the entire bar at one time; rather, it is the constant shifting of the active stream that scours the bed clean of vegetation and soil on a periodic basis.

If the stream course is stable for a number of years, flood-tolerant willow will invade and, by taking root in the shifting gravel, stabilize the soil. These early successional stages of willow will still provide easy walking for the hiker, with firm footing and negligible underbrush. As the willows grow to maturity, however, their branches begin to intertwine, and the brush may become impenetrable.

Generally, however, gravel bars are brush-free and bone dry. The footing is fairly good; hikers need only to worry about unstable cobbles rolling underfoot. Seasoned hikers can count on making 3 miles an hour if the gravel bars are fairly continuous. Wildlife also use gravel bars heavily for travel, sometimes blazing trails through otherwise impenetrable brush. Grizzly bears concentrate their springtime feeding efforts on the roots of peavine, which grows on disturbed sites near rivers. In the fall, soapberry bushes, which also grow on gravel bars, are a top item on the bear's menu. Make extra noise when traveling along game trails and streams where the visibility is low, because the rushing of the water may mask your approach and result in a confrontation with a bear. Caribou also use gravel bars extensively during their seasonal migrations between favorable ranges.

You may also encounter geological barriers during the course of streamside travel. Waterfalls and steep-walled canyons may block your passage in places where the streambed has cut down through hard rock. Do not try to climb around on steep surfaces in these areas, because the walls are often slick with spray, and you don't want to fall into a roiling torrent. It is a much safer strategy to climb onto the surrounding bluffs, and believe it or not, you will actually save time and energy by doing so. And watch out for cut banks where steep slopes of loose dirt may block your passage—generally at the outside of a bend in the stream. The loose dirt provides unstable footing and triggers frequent mudslides. Walking across it can hasten erosion and dump mud into otherwise clear streams. Unless the slope is quite gentle, it is best to avoid traveling on bare dirt. At low water, you can sometimes make a passage on the rocks at the edge of the stream. At high water or where the stream bank is undercut, this will not be possible and it will be necessary to ford the stream or climb the river bluff to get around.

Evaluate all of your traveling options when deciding whether a streamside route is the most practical. It is easy to follow a stream until the going gets difficult, and then abandon it for the higher surrounding slopes. It is certainly a better strategy to hike on the hillsides if you are forced to make a difficult ford every couple of hundred yards. Similarly, if you are always climbing up and down to avoid cut banks, it might be a better plan to just stay up on the bluffs and try to make a passage there. Overall, however, watercourses are often the easiest and fastest highways into the backcountry, and provide ample landmarks to help you find your way.

Hiking Through the Habitats

The Alaskan landscape is a mosaic of varying habitats and plant communities. A practiced eye can read the landscape using the distribution of plant communities as an index to select a safe and efficient route. A party that makes fast time on the cobbles of a river bar would be slowed to a crawl when confronted with tussock tundra. A working knowledge of these plant communities can help you avoid such time-consuming mistakes and permit you to traverse the Alaskan landscape with safety and efficiency.

At the same time, you should know which habitats are sensitive to disturbance and require extra care. Try to confine your route to durable surfaces that will not incur lasting damage as a result of your passage. Hikers traveling in groups should spread themselves in a line abreast wherever possible, rather than following each other in single file. This will prevent the formation of new trails on the virgin landscape (except on the rocky debris at the base of a cliff known as *talus*, where impacts are minimal and hiking single file is safer). In general, tundra habitats with their short growing seasons harbor the most fragile plant communities. Water-saturated soils are damaged most easily, while dry soils are more resistant to compaction and provide more pleasant walking as well. Travel on snow or bare rock wherever this is possible. Hikers can also minimize their impacts by taking rest stops on sturdy sites such as rock outcrops or patches of bare gravel, where there are no plants to be damaged.

Boreal Forest. Boreal forest covers much of the upland country of interior Alaska. It is made up of a mixture of white spruce, aspen, balsam poplar, and paper birch. In the central Yukon, these trees are augmented by species like lodgepole pine and balsam fir that are common in the Rocky Mountains. The understory is typically mossy and lacks extensive underbrush, making for fairly easy walking. Recent burns can be quite brushy, with extensive brakes of willow and fireweed. Boreal forest tends to be well drained on the ridgelines, with swampy permafrost areas in depressions and broad valleys. Visibility is limited because of the trees, so do not expect help from prominent landmarks to aid your navigation.

Boreal Forest

White Spruce. Open stands of white spruce prefer the well-drained, fertile soils found on low ridges and along watercourses. Such habitats are typical of the interior valley bottoms, and can also be found at low elevations in mountainous areas from the Alaska Range northward and east into the Yukon Territories. The trees are typically spaced 20 to 30 yards apart, because competition for nutrients between the broad root systems of neighboring trees prevents young trees from taking root in the openings. The understory vegetation is quite variable, and ranges from dense dwarf birch to scattered willow to lichen and moss. The acidic needles of the spruce trees usually prevent brushy vegetation from getting a foothold close to the trunks of the trees. As a result, hiking through the openings among white spruce is generally quite easy.

The one pitfall to hiking in open spruce habitats is that the trees tend to obscure prominent landmarks, making navigation a challenge. Be aware that it is easy to wander around in circles in a white spruce forest, because everywhere you look the country is about the same. Hikers who travel here should have good map and compass skills.

Open White Spruce Forest

If you are caught out in a cloudburst, mature white spruce trees make excellent umbrellas that will keep you dry until the rain passes. The dense branches of the spruce angle out and down from the trunk, forming a cone shape. The falling rain lands on the branches and obeys the laws of gravity, running downward along each branch until it reaches the tip and drops off. It then lands on the next branch, traveling farther from the base as it follows the branches downward, and so on. As a result, the soft duff at the base of the tree never gets wet, and you can weather substantial storms in perfect comfort if you bivouac at the base of a spruce with branches that droop close to the ground.

Black Spruce Permafrost. Over vast expanses of the Alaskan landscape, low annual temperatures dictate that only the top foot or two of the soil thaws during the brief summer. The underlying frozen soil is called permafrost, because it is permanently frozen. The permafrost provides a hard foundation through which water cannot percolate. As a result, water runoff is extremely slow, and standing water is common. The saturated, supercooled soil near the surface has very few nutrients, because the soil microbes break down organic material more and more slowly as temperatures drop.

The black spruce is the climax, or dominant, plant type on shallow permafrost sites that occur below the treeline. It has an incredibly slow growth rate, and is able to survive on very low-nutrient soils. Stands of black spruce are prevalent in the low basins of interior Alaska and the northern Yukon, and can also be found in poorly drained basins in the mountains.

Black spruce can be separated from white spruce by several characteristics. The black spruce has a characteristic shape that looks for all the world like a popsicle stick with globs of branches stuck on in odd places, while the white spruce has a more stately, uniform, Christmas-tree shape. The cones of the black spruce are round to egg-shaped, while the cones of white spruce are more elongated. White spruce shed their cones, while black spruce retain theirs in clusters near the top of the tree. Because permafrost is very unstable and black spruce have

Black Spruce Permafrost

shallow roots, the trees in this habitat are frequently found leaning crazily in all directions, a phenomenon dubbed "the drunken forest."

Black spruce permafrost sites on the flats are typically damp to boggy, with frequent pools of standing water that make ideal mosquito nurseries. Understory vegetation is typically sparse, and often a thick, spongy moss is all that covers the ground. The soil is often pushed up into a series of 1- or 2-foot-high ridges by the action of the frost, and this makes walking difficult. The areas between the ridges are often filled with water puddles that can be as deep as your waist. Exercise caution when wading through such puddles, because even the smallest ones can soak you. When black spruce is associated with swampy areas, the habitat is called *muskeg*. On the Kenai Peninsula and in southeast Alaska, hardpans of clay can create black spruce muskeg even though permafrost does not form here. If you prefer to keep your feet dry, you should move to higher, well-drained slopes whenever black spruce muskeg is encountered.

Brushy Tundra. Brushy tundra comes in a number of varieties, ranging from easily traversable to impenetrable. This section deals with areas in the drier climates of interior and far northern Alaska; the brush fields above the treeline found in the wetter coastal areas will be discussed later (see "Coastal Brush Fields"). Three types of shrubs make up the bulk of brushy tundra: dwarf birch, willow, and alder. The interspersion of these shrub types in the landscape depends mainly on slope and drainage patterns. Brushy tundra is a dominant habitat type along the skirts of the Alaska Range, and occurs at higher altitudes in the White Mountains and Yukon-Tanana uplands.

Dwarf birch occur primarily on dry sites with firm footing. Dwarf birch are usually between 2 and 3 feet high, although on the North Slope they measure only a few inches off the ground. In some cases, especially on ridgelines, the density of the birch is sparse, with lichens and blueberries occurring in between. Under these circumstances, it is easy to find a path among the

Brushy Tundra

shrubs and make good time across the tundra. If the birch are growing in dense groves, however, forcing a passage can be nearly impossible. The stems of the birch are twisted into odd angles, and many stems stick out horizontally from their root mass, interlocking with other vertical stems. The result is a nest of trip wires that is beastly to cross. When you get stuck in a dense thicket of dwarf birch, go slowly and do not lean too far forward. This will keep you from falling flat on your face when your foot is snagged by one of the offending stems. When seeking a path through dwarf birch, look for the white and pale green color of exposed lichens, which mark brush-free travel corridors with firm footing.

Willow grow in a variety of places, but do best in areas where they have access to plenty of water. As a result, they are often found on poorly drained hillsides and in riparian areas, the floodplains of rivers and streams. The size of willow ranges from knee-high to 10 feet, depending on the species and the quality of the soil. Willow are a favorite food of moose, and as a result, dense willow patches will frequently have moose trails running through them (although these trails may be several feet deep in water). You can usually spot dense willow patches from a distance and navigate to avoid them. Unlike birch, willow have straight stems. As a result, you can swing your feet vigorously through a willow patch and expect them to find the path of least resistance, even when you can't see it from above.

Alder occur in dense clumps that are difficult to penetrate, and are a genuine hassle to get through. The popular term for a thicket of these plants is "alder hell," a moniker that is well deserved. Each plant has many stems that grow outward from a single base, forming a bush shape that at maturity can reach 15 feet in height. If the alder are mature, you can actually move through the interiors of individual clumps. Because the branches tend to lean downslope, it is much easier to walk downhill through such a patch than to traverse it across the slope of the hill. Alder grow thickly in moist ravines in steep country, as well as on disturbed sites such as old roadbeds, mine sites, and avalanche chutes. There is no way to see the country in front of you when you are traveling through an alder hell, so it is a good idea to shout every few yards to warn bears of your presence.

Tussock Tundra. Tussock tundra occurs in patches in the Alaska Range, and occupies broad expanses of the North Slope (between the Brooks Range and the Arctic Ocean). The bane of hikers who venture above treeline, tussock tundra provides miles and miles of misery for hikers who get mired in it. The tussocks themselves are dense clumps of sedges and grasses that grow on elevated pedestals. These pedestals are quite unstable, and if you go hopping from tussock to tussock, eventually one will capsize beneath you. This instability makes tussocks a prime risk for twisting ankles and wrenching knees, so you should place your feet in the low spots between the tussocks to avoid injury.

As if the tussocks themselves weren't bad enough, the spaces between the tussocks are typically filled with water from 6 inches to 2 feet deep. If you wear breakup boots (see Chapter

Tussock Tundra

3), you might get through with dry feet, but otherwise it is pretty difficult to get across an expanse of tussock tundra without going in over your boot tops. Bob Marshall, the father of the American wilderness system, explored the central Brooks Range in 1929. Of tussocks, he wrote, "They are very topheavy, and when you step on them they are almost certain to bend over and pitch you off into the swamp. When you try to walk in the swamp, you have to step over these high humps, and they sometimes grow so close together your foot catches in between."

These swamps have the gravity-defying ability to exist on hillsides as well as on flats, so you can't always avoid them by moving to higher ground. The permafrost often forms terraces on the hillsides, and these trap water for the tussocks. Try to keep away from tussock tundra, because it will slow you down to half a mile per hour, stretching time out until it stands still.

Sedge Meadow with Cottongrass

Sedge Meadows. Sedge meadows are typically found within tundra areas from the Alaska Range northward. Here, far above the treeline, the poorly drained, shallow marshes are invaded by single-stemmed sedges and rushes. Cottongrass is one of the most striking members of the sedge family. It produces a cottony wisp of fibers to carry its seeds on the wind. Like other sedges, it grows only in soils that are saturated with water for much of the year. These sedges do not form clumps, but grow in a uniform pattern in flooded areas, rather like rice in a rice paddy. The mud below them can be mucky, but is typically not deep and offers fair traction. If you don't mind getting your feet wet, sedge meadows offer rapid, safe travel. They are also fairly impact resistant when dry, and make good campsites when rain is not in the forecast.

Mat Tundra. Broad expanses of mat tundra occur on the north slopes of the Ogilvie, Richardson, Alaska, and Brooks Ranges. It is every hiker's dream to walk on: a mixed bag of microhabitats, many of which offer easy and comfortable travel. On moist sites, thick mats of springy moss predominate. Because the moss will give way beneath your feet with each step, you will have to raise your feet much higher than usual, as if you were climbing stairs. As a result, traversing this type of tundra can be rather toilsome. Look for light-colored lichens when traversing moss mats, because they indicate firm, rocky substrate that will not sink underfoot. On drier ridgelines and alluvial fans, lichens and flowering plants are interspersed with grasses. Here, the mat-tundra footing is firm and the miles slide by effortlessly. This type of habitat makes for easy walking, but extra care should be taken to avoid damaging it in your passage.

A related plant community known as alpine tundra can be found above 3000 feet in the Wrangell and Talkeetna Mountains and in the ranges along the southern coast of Alaska. These tundras offer displays of delicate wildflowers throughout the season, and patches of the delicious dwarf blueberry ripen in early autumn. Arctic shrubs that grow prostrate along the ground are found here, and provide fiery displays of fall colors.

Mat Tundra

Bear in mind that herbaceous mat tundra and alpine tundra may be easily damaged, especially if the underlying soil is waterlogged. Mat tundra that is typified by dwarf willow, mountain avens, and kinnikinnick is more impact resistant and makes a good camping surface.

Coastal Forest. In southeast and south-central Alaska, the presence of moisture-laden air has led to a lush rainforest community dominated by Sitka spruce, hemlock, and cedar. In old-growth forests, the trees are widely spaced, and there is virtually no understory vegetation. Green moss clings to the lower branches of trees, and a thin, springy layer of moss on the forest floor makes travel easy. Regenerating forests up to the pole size, as are found in clearcuts or burns, are dense and difficult to penetrate. Similarly, forest openings are often choked with brush and provide difficult traveling. For best results, try to

Coastal Forest

stick to ridgelines, which are well drained and thus less likely to provide obstacles.

Coastal Brush Field. Coastal habitats above timberline (between 1000 and 2000 feet) and in avalanche chutes are typified by dense brush, highlighted by elderberry, alder, and similar delights. Also included in the bargain is devil's club, a spiny (but not poisonous) plant that resembles salmonberry. Visibility in coastal brush fields is zero, which gives you the added problem of warning bears in your path of your impending arrival. All in all, bushwhacking through coastal brush fields is for masochists, and more practical hikers should choose other routes.

Coastal Brush Field

6 Special Travel Techniques

THE Alaskan wilderness is an unforgiving place. Those who venture forth unprepared rarely escape misfortune, and in this country misfortune can be deadly. You should become as familiar as possible with the obstacles and dangers facing you, for in this great land, familiarity breeds respect. The varied landscape of Alaska provides both hazards and safe havens, obstacles and opportunities. Those who take the time to learn about the landscape will reap the benefits that come from intimacy with the environment, while the ignorant are in for a rough time. This chapter will familiarize you with many of the challenges you will encounter, as well as providing techniques for dealing with them successfully. Bear in mind, however, that this book cannot hope to give foolproof solutions to every difficult situation. Nothing beats personal experience and creativity when dealing with challenging obstacles.

Stream Crossings

Alaska receives its fair share of precipitation, mostly in the form of winter snows. As a result, backcountry travel usually includes frequent creek and river crossings. Most of the Alaskan wilderness is completely lacking in developed trails, and even in areas that have trails, high water levels at spring runoff often preclude the building of bridges. As a result, it won't take long for most hikers to get their feet wet in the course of backcountry travels. Confidence in stream crossings comes with prac-

Glacial river, with braided channels characteristic of mountain streams

tice, but here are some pointers to help you traverse watercourses without going for an involuntary bath.

Timing Is Everything

If you can plan your stream crossings to coincide with times of low water, they will be easier and less dangerous. Spring runoff happens from early May to late June, depending on the locality, and watercourses are deluged with turbulent, flood-level waters. Rivers are for the most part impossible to cross during this time, and even small streams can pose potential hazards for the unwary. Later on, in July, water levels tend to drop and water clarity improves, which may allow you to see where you are going.

Streams that originate from glaciers will always be too silty to see through, and crossing glacial streams will have you reading the stream bottom in braille in no time. Water levels in glacial streams depend more on air temperature than on recent rainfall: A succession of hot days will cause the glacier to melt more rapidly, causing water levels to rise. However, these streams also rise quickly in response to rainstorms, because they typically lack the vegetation cover that helps to slow the runoff. Because the silt blocks sunlight and scours the streambed on a continuous basis, slippery rocks are usually not a problem in watercourses of glacial origin. If you're crossing a lot of glacial streams, pray for cloudy and cool weather, which makes for the lowest possible water levels.

Streams not of glacial origin rise quickly following downpours, and tend to remain high for several days after the rain has ceased. The size of the watershed also determines how severe the high water will be. Tiny streams that drain large areas often grow dramatically in size, while larger streams with relatively small watersheds may barely rise following a rainstorm. Clearwater streams pose an additional hazard in that streambed cobbles are often coated with slimy algae, which thrive in the abundant sunlight and provide a slippery surface for walking.

On a daily basis, it is almost always wise to schedule your most challenging stream crossings for the morning hours. Temperatures drop during the evening hours, causing snowbanks to melt more slowly. As a result, the lowest water levels of the day typically occur before 10 in the morning unless a storm has passed during the night.

Reading the Water

Like the trout angler, the Arctic traveler should learn to "read the water"—that is, learn to interpret the water's surface characteristics and what they imply about the depth and speed of the water underneath. In a basic sense, riffles, or areas of choppy water on moderate slopes, are characterized by shallow water that is moving fairly rapidly. By contrast, the surface water of a run can be quite glassy, but by watching the subtle roils on the surface, you will be able to determine that the water is running at quite a rapid clip. Runs occur on moderately sloped segments of watercourses, and are dangerous because their water is comparatively deep and flows rapidly downhill, unimpeded by current-slowing rocks or logs. Large rocks in the midst of runs and riffles create eddies behind them, which express themselves at the surface as slicks of flat water extending downstream from the obstruction. These eddies are safe havens from the current, as their water is essentially still.

Pools occur where the streambed reaches flat areas, and are slow moving and can be quite deep. Pools tend to be deepest at their upper end, where riffles and runs enter with great force, scooping out a deep basin. They gradually become shallower, until the slope of the streambed steepens again and the pool tumbles off into another riffle. In a given stretch of river, it is generally best to seek out the lower border of a pool as your crossing point, because the water there is typically broad, shallow, and slow moving. It frequently makes sense to cross streams at their broadest point, because velocity tends to decrease as the water spreads out over a greater area; this also results in shallower water to cross.

In mountainous areas, streams and rivers frequently have braided sections where the main channel divides into many smaller channels. This phenomenon occurs where fast-moving streams pass over streambeds of loose cobbles, which are pushed about continuously by the current. As the water bulldozes piles of rocks it dams its own flow, and the water obeys the law of gravity and seeks a lower path. Braided areas are the most favorable places to cross a river, because they reduce the main channel to many small stream crossings. Try to cross the greatest number of individual channels possible. The greater the number of channels, the less water flow in each, and thus the greater the ease in crossing. It is useful to note that the places where one channel splits into two are often favorable crossing points, because the stream banks of the original single channel remain, providing you with a shallow walkway.

Crossing Techniques

Upon reaching the water's edge, most hikers are immediately assailed by a dread of plunging into near-freezing water. Your crossing will seem even colder if you try to make your ford barefooted. Since most folks don't like to hike around in wet boots all day, I recommend bringing a pair of canvas shoes specifically for the purpose of fording streams. Even these thin coverings will prevent heat loss to the cold stream cobbles, and will improve your traction for a safer crossing. Wearing neoprene booties or socks inside your shoes is another method to keep your feet warm, if not dry, during the crossing.

Walking staffs, which are useless for most other purposes, add additional stability when wading streams. Some outdoor companies manufacture metal-tipped staffs for wading, and some of these even telescope down to packable proportions. The best way to support yourself with a staff is to grip the wood in both hands and angle the bottom of the staff downstream. This way, you can brace yourself against the force of the current. If you use a staff to aid your crossing, remember not to lean too hard on it; your legs should always bear most of your weight.

Before entering the stream, unclip your hip belt and other restrictive straps so that you can shed your pack in case you fall into the river. If you get into a situation where you have to bail out of your pack, having the straps unclipped could save you from drowning. Knee-deep water can usually be forded without much difficulty; midthigh is the maximum safe depth for crossing if there is a substantial current to contend with. Once you get in up to your hips, your body offers the current a broad profile to push against, and you can bet that it won't be long before you are swimming.

When wading, discipline yourself to take tiny steps. The water will be cold, and your first impulse will be to rush across and get warm again, but this kind of carelessness frequently results in a dunking. While inching your way across, your feet should be seeking the lowest possible footing, so that it is impossible to slip downward any farther. It is useful to advance

FIGURE 4. *When making a stream crossing, remember to have your hip belt unclipped and to take small steps. Knee-deep water can usually be forded without much difficulty.*

your upstream foot first, then bring the downstream foot up into the eddy formed behind your upstream leg. Folks who try to stride across the current, alternating their lead foot, provide a broader profile for the curent to push against and thus are more susceptible to being overturned. Use submerged boulders as braces for your feet; these rocks will have tiny underwater eddies on their upstream and downstream sides that will reduce the force of the current against your legs. When emerging from the water, dry off as quickly as possible with a towel or other absorbent piece of cloth. If you allow the water to evaporate from your skin, it will take with it additional heat that your body could have used to warm itself.

If you do fall in the water, your first action should be to shuck your pack. It can only act as an anchor to drag you down, and you can chase it downstream once you are back on land. If the water is deep, float on your back with your feet pointed downstream to fend off boulders. Using your arms to do a sort of elementary backstroke, swim across the stream to reach the safety of the shoreline. Once you have salvaged your pack, change immediately into dry clothes for warmth.

If you are traveling in a large group, a safer and more stable method for crossing is to break into groups of three and form triads. The three hikers should grasp their comrades around the shoulders, forming a united triangle with all facing inward. The linked triad can then shuffle across the stream, supporting one another in case of slips or heavy water. The strongest of the three should be upstream, so that the other two occupy the eddy created by the wake of the upstream member. It is still important that all members of the triad unclip their packs and be ready to shed them in case of calamity.

You can also employ a walking staff as a handrail for group crossings. Form a line along the river's edge, shoulder to shoulder, with each hiker holding the staff at waist level. The strongest person should be at the upstream end of the line, with weaker hikers sandwiched between strong ones for extra support. The whole line can then wade across the stream, staying parallel to the current so that only the upstream hiker takes the brunt of the flow. Let the shortest person determine the exact pace, which should be slow and cautious.

Some streams will be narrow and shallow, with boulders that protrude above the surface of the water and beckon you to hopscotch across without getting your feet wet. Be careful, because this is a prime ankle-spraining situation. Damp rocks often have a film of slippery algae on them, and even dry rocks may be unstable and roll out from underfoot. To avoid calamity, set foot only onto boulders that are completely dry, and never jump onto an untested boulder. The best policy is to keep one foot on a solid base at all times, so that you have a firm foothold to fall back on in case the next rock proves to be unstable. If the rock-hopping gets too difficult, revert to wading. After all, it is better to have wet feet than a sprained ankle.

Overflow Ice

In the spring and fall, temperatures are frequently cold enough to freeze rapidly running streams solid in a matter of days. The freezing patterns of the stream are much different in the extreme cold of Alaska than they are in the lower 48 and deserve some special attention. Once a stream freezes for the winter, the remaining water flowing beneath the ice begins to erode away the lower surface. Water levels then drop as the available water becomes locked up as ice and snow, leaving substantial gaps between water and ice. Periodic warm spells can melt large amounts of snow, significantly raising the level of the streams. The swollen stream may break through its frozen surface and begin flowing on top of the ice. This water then refreezes— sometimes solidly, sometimes only on the surface.

Such overflow ice can form on streams of all sizes, even on the largest of rivers, and makes a treacherous surface for crossings. Use extreme caution when crossing frozen streams, because the surface may give way at any time, plunging you into the icy water below. Hypothermia and broken bones are a frequent result of such encounters with frozen streams. For your own safety, be aware of the danger: If you must cross, do so with the utmost caution, testing the ice ahead of you with a walking stick or other heavy object.

In the depths of winter, the stream may also begin to freeze from the bottom up, forming slippery anchor ice on the streambed. This condition often persists late into spring, when it can ambush the unwary at a stream crossing. There is no good technique for avoiding slippage when crossing a stream with anchor ice in it. It is better to avoid the anchor ice altogether by crossing in a steady riffle, where anchor ice is slow to form and is quickly melted away by the fast-flowing water.

Negotiating Scree and Talus Slopes

Yet another challenge facing backcountry travelers are the rocky inclines known as scree and talus slopes. The actions of weathering are continually at work on the rock faces of mountains. Water seeps into cracks and crevices in the living rock, then freezes and expands, acting as a wedge to split off chunks of material ranging from the size of a pea to a house. This process is known as frost cracking and results in broad aprons of loose rock material called *talus* and *scree* at the feet of mountain faces. These slopes of loose material are a challenge to cross, and can be quite dangerous. In general, it is best to avoid them entirely.

Scree is formed when naturally crumbly igneous and sedimentary rocks break into tiny fragments. When crossing a scree slope, it is not unusual to cause a miniature landslide with every step. Some folks are big fans of scree skiing, which is done by glissading downhill through the loose gravel, holding the feet stationary. This is a dangerous practice, because you tend to build up speed rather quickly, and unseen pieces of bedrock beneath the scree can catch your feet and send you flying downhill. When descending a scree slope, I prefer to adopt a rolling gait, letting the scree give way a bit beneath each step, and allowing my momentum to carry me along. If you take a path that is diagonal to the fall line, rather than going straight across the slope, you will minimize the chances of starting a rockslide. If Dall sheep are in the area, look for evidence of

Talus slopes are characterized by unstable boulders.

sheep trails across the scree, and step where the sheep have; sheep have an instinctive sense of where the scree is stable and thus will stick to safe footing.

Rubble larger than a grapefruit is called talus. Talus is usually made of harder metamorphic rock such as granite. Because the larger rocks tend to interlock with each other, and weigh a lot, talus slopes tend to be more stable than scree. Nevertheless, when hiking across talus, be aware that rocks may roll underfoot at any time, and ankle sprains are a definite possibility. Groups crossing a talus slope should space themselves out in a single file. This way, nobody will get hurt in the event of a dislodged boulder or a rockslide. Look for paths within the talus slope where moss grows among the boulders; this indicates rock that has remained stable for a long period of time.

In general, unstable surfaces ranging from dirt embankments to boulder fields are to be avoided if possible. A good rule of thumb is, If it has vegetation growing on it, I can walk there. Because Alaska has a short growing season and harsh weather, vegetation takes a long time to grow, and can never really get a start if the soil is always sliding downhill. Thus, the presence of vegetation on a hillside indicates stable soil. Remember, however, that even vegetation-covered hillsides can be slippery following rain or snow.

Snowfield Travel

In many parts of the Far North, snow is the only walking surface available for 7 months out of the year, and many snowfields persist throughout the summer. Winter snows begin to disappear in May throughout most of the state, and by late June, snow has disappeared from all but the high country. Because backpackers tend to seek out high places, they are often faced with crossing snowfields of varying pitch and hardness. Expect to find snowfields along the north sides of ridges, in bowl-shaped depressions on ridgetops, in the bottoms of steep ravines, and close to active glaciers.

Special Equipment

Snowshoes and cross-country skis are the travel modes of choice if snow is still widespread, but it really doesn't make sense to carry these unwieldy items if the snow is present only in patches. There is, however, some equipment that is portable and will help make traversing snowy areas safer and easier.

Ice axes are versatile tools that can be employed to prevent falls on steep snow, and to stop your slide if a fall occurs. (Appropriate techniques are discussed in the following sections.) Ice axes were originally heavy affairs, with wooden handles and steel blades. Modern ice axes use lightweight alloy blades and have shafts of plastic polymer. You may see short-handled ice axes in specialty shops; they are designed for ice climbing and are of little value to hikers. If you intend to use your ax for preventing falls and arresting slides while hiking on snow, you should get one that is long enough so that the shaft point touches the ground while you are standing erect, with your arm slightly bent.

Crampons are sets of spikes that attach to your boots, and are used frequently by mountaineers. They can be quite useful for glacier travel, and provide stable footing on the slippery surface of the ice. Flexible crampons are adequate for crossing glaciers below the firn line, or the lower boundary of the accumulation zone (see "Glacial Topography," page 134). However, if you are traveling on slopes that are steep enough to require crampons to cross, you are on technical terrain requiring mountaineering skills. Not only should your party have the requisite gear such as ropes and mountaineering harnesses, but it should also possess all the expertise that such equipment entails. Summer avalanches may be encountered by mountaineers, but are a rare occurrence on nontechnical slopes. Thus, I will leave the discussion of avalanche safety and equipment to other sources.

At high altitudes, the earth's atmosphere is thinner, providing less protection from harmful ultraviolet (UV) rays. This problem is compounded where snow is present, since the rays from the sun and those reflected from the snow's surface combine to give you a double dose of radiation. Protect yourself by bringing along a good pair of sunglasses that filter out UV light. Fair-skinned folk should also bring along sunscreen, and lip balm with sunscreen is a must for all hikers, as the lips tend to dry out and burn easily at high elevations.

Making Your Crossing

Snow conditions change seasonally, weekly, and daily. Before you go out, find out if you can expect to encounter much snow, so that you can prepare yourself mentally and assemble the right equipment. Remember that snowfields warm up and begin to melt during the day, and may freeze again at night. A snow crust that will support a hiker in the morning may melt by noon, leaving you to flounder through waist-deep drifts, a miserable experience at best. When crossing flat snowfields, firm snow makes for easier trekking, while steeper snowfields are crossed more easily when the snow is softer.

When crossing a steep snowfield, first assess your options. Ask yourself: Is there another route if I climb or descend a ways? If I start sliding, will the pitch of the snowfield slow my slide or will I keep accelerating, only to be flung off a cliff or onto a pile of rocks?

As someone who has taken slides that have dropped me over ledges, I can tell you that before you start crossing, you should be certain that you can stop yourself if you fall. If you can't, you should look for another route to get where you are going.

Be aware that streams may be flowing beneath the snow. Where this occurs, the snow melts from underneath, forming snow bridges that appear stable but may only be a few inches thick. Since nobody likes to fall through and get soaked with icy water, it is wise to look around the snowbank for incoming streams before crossing.

When starting across, kick stairs into the snow using the toes of your boots. Other members of your party can use these same holes, enlarging them with the kicking motions of their own feet.

And use existing animal or human tracks in the snow where they are available, as they indicate that the snow is stable and will support your weight. If necessary, you can drive your open hands into the snow to provide additional stability. In this fashion, you should be able to cross most snowfields without difficulty. The following sections cover two techniques that are especially useful in preventing falls and arresting slides on snow.

Self-Belay. Self-belay permits you to use your ice ax as a portable snow anchor to provide a stable handhold in case you slip. To execute a self-belay, plant your feet firmly in the snow. The ice ax should be gripped so that your thumb and forefinger encircle the pick blade. With the ax held in this manner, you can drive the haft straight down into the snow, with the heel of your hand exerting downward force on the adze blade of the ice ax. Once the haft is driven securely into the snow, you can move forward several steps, then remove the ax and drive it into position for your next steps. If you slip, put one hand on the ax head and one hand on the shaft where it enters the snow. By putting most of your weight near the snow's surface, you will minimize the chances that the ice ax will be levered out of the snow by the force of your fall (see Figure 5A).

Self-Arrest. If you will be crossing snowfields that have even a moderate slope, slipping is a serious concern, and you must carry an ice ax in hand to self-arrest in case of a fall. The narrow, toothed blade of the ice ax is specially designed to be driven into the snow as a brake to slow your descent to a halt.

To self-arrest after beginning a downhill slide, first roll over onto your stomach. Then push the narrow blade of the ice ax into the surface of the snow with steady pressure. Avoid driving the blade in suddenly; if it grabs the ice, the force of your slide will tear the ax from your grasp. Instead, lean on the ax with the entire weight of your upper body, gradually digging the ax in deeper and using friction to halt the slide. Keep your upper arms close to your sides so that the ax head is near your head. This will allow you to bring all of your weight to bear (see Figure 5B).

FIGURE 5A. *In the self-belay, which is a good technique to use on snowfields with even a moderate slope, you drive your ice ax into the snow to provide a stable handhold in case you begin to slip.*

FIGURE 5B. *The self-arrest technique is used to stop a fall on a snowfield. This hiker stops his head-downward skid by using the ice ax as a brake and as a lever to return to the head-upward position.*

Self-Arrest Grip

Self-Belay Grip

FIGURE 6.

The proper way to carry the ice ax while hiking is to grip the handle just below the head, or to grip the head itself where it joins the handle. Many packs these days have special loops near the bottom that allow you to stow the ice ax conveniently when it is not in use (see Figure 6 for the proper grips for self-belay and self-arrest).

Novices should practice the self-arrest on a gentle, safe slope before attempting to cross steeper snowfields. Choose a snow hill with a gradual runout, so that you will not have a long slide if you fail to self-arrest. Start out by practicing the self-arrest from the simplest position, with your head facing upslope. When you have mastered this proposition, learn to self-arrest from a head-downward skid. To accomplish this feat, drag the point of the ax in the snow, and let your greater speed work against the friction of the tool until your feet swing to the downslope side. Once this position is attained, self-arrest as for the head-upward position.

Glacier Travel

Glaciers are huge rivers of ice that flow from high mountain areas toward the valleys below. They form when winter snowfall in the mountains exceeds summer melting. The newly accumulated snow eventually presses down on the older snow beneath, compressing it and transforming it into ice. Under tons of pressure, the ice becomes plastic and begins to flow downhill at a rate that may exceed half a mile per year, but typically is much less. Several valley glaciers may flow together to form one large, flowing mass of ice, called a *trunk glacier*.

As the glacier flows down the valley, it carves the rock below and around it, adding the debris to its moving mass. Most of this debris is loosened by plucking, not scouring: The friction of movement causes the ice to melt, and as it refreezes, it binds protruding rocks into its mass. Bands of rock debris can often be seen running the length of the glacier, and toward the *terminus,* or foot of the glacier, the ice mass may be entirely coated with rubble. At the terminus and along the sides, the rubble is deposited as ridges of loose gravel known as *moraines.* In places where two glaciers converge, a long strip of rubble called a *medial moraine* may be present in the center of the combined ice flow.

When the climate warms, the glacier retreats, leaving a characteristic U-shaped valley with a flat floor and steep walls. Glaciers running parallel to each other often shave the intervening ridge into a narrow knife edge known as an *arête.* Protruding peaks that bear glaciers on three or more faces become scalloped into sharp points known as *horn peaks.* Glaciers often carry huge boulders along as they flow downhill, and deposit them at random as the ice retreats. These boulders are known as *glacial erratics* because they are found far from their parent rock.

At first glance, glacier surfaces appear to be safe and rapid highways to the inner peaks. Upon closer inspection, however, you will find that glaciers pose a number of dangers and difficulties that may make you want to look elsewhere for a travel

Eroded spires of ice at the foot of Exit Glacier, in Kenai Fjords

corridor. Captain Edwin Glenn of the US Army crossed the foot of a glacier during his exploration of south-central Alaska in 1899. His journal contains the following passage: "At one or two places, upon coming to the top of a rise and looking over, I found myself gazing down to a depth of from 100 to 300 feet through an opening in the glacier, where I could see and hear the raging torrent below and feel my hair gradually but surely lifting my hat." More recently, one of America's most talented and experienced mountaineers, Mugs Stump, met an untimely end while traveling on the Kahiltna Glacier in Denali National Park. Glacier travel is dangerous business, and should only be attempted by mountaineers. If you do decide to travel on glacial surfaces, be sure to bring along at least one person skilled in crevasse rescue to be your guide as you make your crossing.

Glacial Topography

Glaciers and ice caps can be broadly divided into two zones based on the trend of snow deposition: the accumulation zone and the melting zone. The accumulation zone occurs at the head of the glacier, where snow deposition exceeds melting. Snowfields typically cover the ice here, masking crevasses under blankets of new powder. This is treacherous country, and should be attempted only by mountaineers. When venturing into the accumulation zone, *each member* of the climbing party must have completed a course in crevasse rescue to ensure the safety of the group. The lower boundary of the accumulation zone is called the *firn line,* and below it lies the melting zone. Snowmelt exceeds snow deposition on an annual basis, and thus the ice is exposed during summertime. The dangers are more obvious here, but parties should still rope up and bring along a seasoned guide.

One of the most prominent and dangerous features of the glacier landscape is the crevasse. Crevasses form wherever the ice changes direction or speed. This can happen as it goes around curves in the valley, forming radial crevasses. As the glacier rounds a curve, the ice on the inside is compressed, while the ice on the outside of the curve is stretched, forming large cracks. A resistant outcrop of rock beneath the glacier can stimulate crevasse formation as the ice forms a bulge in flowing over it. Finally, crevasses can form along the glacier margin in a herringbone pattern as friction slows the flow of the ice where it meets the rock walls that contain it.

In places where a glacier takes a rapid downward bend, the ice splinters across the entire width of the glacier, forming what is known as an icefall. Icefalls are completely impassable, because the deep rifts and jumbled blocks of ice called *seracs* are tilted at crazy angles, and one misstep can send you hurtling to your doom. These slabs of ice are often unstable, and the weight of a single climber may cause a 100-ton pillar of ice to tumble over. When you encounter an icefall, proceed to the margin of the glacier and try to make a passage up the lateral moraine, a ridge of glacial debris that forms along the edge of the moving ice mass. If you cannot force a passage in this manner, it is wiser to turn back than to risk your neck.

Many glaciers have standing and running water on their surfaces in the form of pools, lakes, and streams. Be especially aware that the presence of water on the surface of the glacier may indicate melting of the glacier as a whole. Below the surface, glaciers are honeycombed with rifts and ice caves, some of which carry running water. Surface water may also pool on the glacier in the form of slick watercourses worn into the ice. These streams typically dive beneath the surface at treacherous caves called *moulins,* where the water churns and froths before plunging deep into the heart of the glacier. Folks who slide down into one of these ice caves find that it is almost impossible to crawl back out. Do not attempt to explore ice caves or moulins, even if they look safe. Their labyrinthine nature makes it easy to lose your sense of direction and become lost.

Ridges of rock debris in the center and along the sides of a glacier provide good travel corridors that are less likely to expose you to the perils of crevasses. Be aware that the ice may lie just below the surface of the loose rock, causing slips for the unwary. Keep a lookout for sand and pea-sized gravel patches in meltwater—these may indicate the presence of thin spots in the surface of the ice. The toes of many valley glaciers in Alaska are covered with debris and sometimes even living tundra. They may nevertheless be pocked with crevasses, moulins, and canyons, so approach them with caution.

The toe of the glacier is a most dangerous area. Unstable blocks of ice may periodically break free from the main mass and tumble downward with crushing force. This calving of the glacier can be fun to watch from a distance, but presents a deadly hazard to explorers who foolishly venture close to the base of the ice.

Special Equipment

It is absolutely essential to rope up while crossing a glacier, in order to increase your odds of survival if a snow bridge collapses or the lip of a crevasse crumbles underfoot. Familiarity with climbing harnesses and their use is a must, and an expert should come along to ensure that all knots are double-checked for proper holding power. And always bring a mountaineering rope with a known history. Climbing ropes are rated by the number of falls that they can withstand before they snap. A rope with an unknown history should always be assumed to have already taken its maximum number of falls, and should be left behind. Optimal spacing for glacier travel is 50 feet between party members. The rope should be kept taut so that any unexpected falls through the ice will be short ones.

Crampons should also be employed when engaging in glacier travel. A good pair of crampons will have spikes not only on the soles but also projecting from the front and sides. This allows the wearer to drive his toes into the surface of an ice slope, gaining traction for ascending and descending. Crampons also provide anchor power for party members when one of the party starts to fall; without them, the entire string would get pulled into the fall.

An ice ax is another useful and necessary tool for glacier travel. At the base of the shaft, it has a triangular spike that can be driven into the ice so that the ice ax can be used as a walking staff. The broad adze blade can be used for carving stairs in the snow. The narrow, sharper pick blade is serrated so that it can be driven into an ice wall when climbing a steep incline, and for self-arresting when sliding down a slope (see "Snowfield Travel"). During the course of glacier travel, climbers should be prepared to instantly drop onto the ice in self-arrest if a party member breaks through the surface.

Negotiating Crevasses

Crevasses can range from a few feet to hundreds of feet in depth, and are often too wide to cross safely. The edges of crevasses are often undercut, and as a result ice that appears to be solid may only be a few inches thick. It is an ironclad rule that you should avoid walking near the lip of a crevasse, lest it crumble under your weight and send you tumbling into the abyss, to be crushed by falling blocks of ice.

The methods of crossing crevasses, in order of desirability

and safety, are as follows. The best method is to travel laterally along the crevasse (keeping well away from the lip) until reaching the solid ice at its end. This end-run strategy is by far the easiest and least dangerous method for making a passage of a crevasse. If this is not an option, climbers may attempt a snow-bridge crossing. Crevasses are often covered in the winter by blankets of snow, and with the approach of spring, the snow melts in an irregular pattern, forming snow bridges that span crevasses. Snow bridges are often thin and unstable, and each one should be tested thoroughly with an ice ax handle or other such probe at all points during the crossing before any weight is put on them. Snow bridges can be quite deceptive: If they completely cover a crevasse, you will never even know that you are passing over a dropoff. Watch for sunken snow that may mask a hidden rift. During the course of glacier travel, it is essential to probe the surface ahead of you constantly so that you can discover hidden crevasses and navigate around them.

Finally, if the crevasse cannot be avoided and no snow bridges are present, climbers may attempt to leap across the breach. While other party members anchor themselves to the ice, climbers should leap singly, with ice ax held ready for self-arrest upon landing. Other party members should position themselves on belay. This technique is exceedingly dangerous, and should only be attempted if all party members are well versed in crevasse rescue.

Scrambling Skills

I do not advocate rock-face ascents to anyone but the pure mountaineer. Folks who venture out onto steep faces are exposing themselves to serious risks, and thus should use the proper techniques and equipment. Most of Alaska is accessible without resorting to the hazards of mountaineering, and so there is very little reason to expose yourself to these risks while hiking or backpacking. Never attempt any sort of climbing while you are by yourself; fatal injuries frequently result from wounds that would have been treatable had another person been there to help. Still, many of the techniques used by rock climbers might prove useful to backpackers in a variety of situations. This section will discuss a few of the more important climbing skills.

First of all, you should become familiar with the properties of the rock you find yourself on. Metamorphic rocks, such as granite, have been smelted in the hot furnace of the earth's mantle into solid, firm rock. These rocks hold up well underfoot, and thus are favored by rock climbers. Igneous rock, which is composed of cooled varieties of magma, crumbles away easily in irregular patterns; it is known as "rotten rock" as a result. It is avoided by climbers because of its instability, which makes it an unsafe climbing surface. Sedimentary rock, formed from old lake, riverbed, and ocean-floor sediments, tends to fracture along the plane in which it was laid down. You should be aware that large chunks of seemingly solid rock can come away in your hand easily and without warning. Exercise extreme caution on all rock surfaces, and always attempt to return to safer footing as quickly as possible.

Balance is basic to any sort of climbing, and if you find yourself in a precarious position, maintaining your balance will be your first concern. Try to keep a low center of gravity by leaning into the slope and keeping your hips close to the slope's surface. By doing so, you can make gravity work for you, pulling you into the safety of the surface rather than away from it. Keep three points (hands, feet) on solid holds at all times while you use the free fourth point to prospect for the next hold. This way, if you can't find a stable hold, you will be able to remain on the rock with the three good holds that you already have.

There are several specialized ways to achieve handholds and footholds on a rock surface. The first is to find fissures in the rock and to slide your hands or feet into the fissures until they are wedged in. Make a finger wedge by holding your open hand straight out from your body, then flexing your fingers (not your whole hand) until they touch their bases. As you look at your closed fingers, notice that they form an almost triangular shape when viewed from the top, with the base of the triangle farthest from your body. This shape is ideal for wedging your fingers into a small crack that widens as it goes deeper into the rock.

The same principle applies to a fist wedge, which is achieved by making a fist with your thumb on top. This wedge can be effective for slightly larger fissures. A foot wedge can also be used by turning your foot inward (so that your sole is vertical) while sticking it into the fissure, then twisting it back to its normal horizontal orientation to lock it into place. All of these wedges will give you scrapes and small cuts; these are the price you will have to pay for scrambling around on the rock.

If you can find a fissure that is wide enough to admit your entire body, you can engage in chimneying, which is a sort of whole-body wedge. If you can reach the back of the fissure, orient yourself to face outward, with hand- and footholds on each side of the opening. Next, use your arms and legs alternately—one pair bracing while the other pair pushes upward or downward—to safely inchworm your way up or down the fissure. If the fissure has no back wall that you can reach, you will need to brace yourself with your back on one wall and your lower legs and hands on the opposite wall, and proceed from there. This form of chimneying tends to be more demanding, because it is more difficult to lock your arms from this position. If you start to cramp up at any time, don't panic. Just wedge yourself in tightly and give your muscles a rest. Soon they will recover, and you will be ready to proceed.

As you travel along, bear in mind that it is always easier and safer to ascend than to descend. This is because on ascent the next handholds will be slightly above eye level, but on descent, a steep pitch will often find you groping blindly with your feet for the next foothold. Avoid being overambitious when climbing, because an error in judgment is as likely to cause injury as discomfort.

Hiking in the Intertidal Zone

Intertidal means between the tides. The intertidal zone is the part of the coastline that is exposed only at low tide. When hiking in coastal areas, intertidal zones can provide relatively easy, brush-free hiking. In places where the mountain cliffs reach the sea, tidal flats at the bases of cliffs may be the *only* way to get around effectively. But timing is of the essence: Because of Alaska's far northern latitude, the magnitude of the tides is accentuated, with tidal flux (the difference in water level between high and low tide) commonly reaching 20 vertical feet. Some of the longer inlets of coastal Alaska experience tidal bores, or standing waves that course inland at a high rate of speed with the incoming tide. These waves can be up to 6 feet high, and can move up a cove at speeds of as much as 12 miles per hour. If you are planning to hike in intertidal areas, carry a tide table with you. Tide tables show the times of high and low tide for each day of the month, and are available from most sporting goods stores near the coast. Inquire locally for special tide conditions before you set out on a coastal hike.

Mud flats present the most common hazard of intertidal zones. Tidal flats frequently are covered with a sticky goo that swallows feet and will not let go. Sucking muds have been known to act like quicksand to trap persons while the tide rushes in to drown them. Stick to pebble and cobble surfaces when hiking in the intertidal zone, as these represent firm footing.

Another intertidal hazard is rock algae. The fertile marine waters foster the growth of all kinds of simple plants, which cover rocks with a slippery mat, making footing treacherous. Vibram soles provide no traction on such a surface. Plan ahead to avoid scrambling about on rock outcrops at low tide.

In rocky areas, the outgoing tide may strand pockets of salt water in the folds of the stone. These tide pools are home to a rich and diverse fauna of mollusks, crustaceans, and other marine creatures. They form a delicately balanced microcosm of the marine ecosystem, and are subjected to extremes of temperature, salinity, and desiccation found nowhere else on earth. The inhabitants of this extreme environment are living on the edges of their survival abilities, and the slightest disturbance can be deadly to them. Look in on these beautiful and fascinating creatures as they make their daily rounds, but don't disturb them.

Respecting the Cold

When most people think about cold in Alaska, frostbite is one of the first things that spring to mind. The body responds to cold temperatures by constricting the blood vessels at the skin's surface and in the extremities so that precious body heat carried in the blood is not lost to the outside environment. This concentrates the warmth in the body core, where it maintains the life-support functions of the fragile innards. As a result of the reduced blood to the skin and extremities, the temperature of these areas drops to low levels. When tissue drops below 28 degrees Fahrenheit, ice crystals begin to form inside the individual cells of the affected area. These ice crystals then expand, bursting cell membranes and causing the extensive tissue damage that is known as frostbite.

The symptoms of frostbite are numbness in the affected area and a pallid white color to the tissue. If the tissue is killed, permanent nerve damage is the rule, and the affected area, if an extremity, may have to be amputated. If you think that you are getting frostbite, cover the affected area and stick it in a warm place. For example, your hands can be stuck into your armpits for warmth, while toes can be warmed in the cleft behind the knee. Do not rub the affected area under any circumstances, because this action merely accelerates the breakup of cell membranes, further damaging the tissue. For the most part, summer weather in Alaska is too warm for frostbite, and it is only the occasional cold snap that poses a real danger.

A far more real danger associated with cold weather is hypothermia. When you start to become cold, your metabolism speeds up to create more heat and maintain the temperature of your body at a constant level. Once the temperature of your body core drops below a critical point, however, the very organs that are responsible for maintaining body warmth are impaired, and you are unable to warm yourself again. When this occurs, the body temperature spirals downward until the brain cools enough to fail.

It doesn't have to be cold outside for hypothermia to set in. In fact, a steady drizzle at 50 degrees is perfect hypothermia weather. Water has an incredible thermal mass, or ability to absorb heat. A thin layer of water next to your skin can rob your body of heat at an amazing rate. It is therefore critical to stay dry in cool weather, and to dry off quickly if you get soaked. If you are wet, stay out of the wind, because a brisk breeze over your wet body will accelerate the cooling of your body temperature through windchill and evaporation of water. Exhaustion, hunger, and dehydration can also accelerate the process of losing body heat. In foul weather, you should maintain a reasonable pace and snack frequently to keep blood sugar levels high.

You can prevent hypothermia by wearing the proper clothing for the weather conditions. Layers work best: Extra clothing can be added and taken off as the need arises, so that you keep warm without breaking into a sweat. Be sure that the clothing next to your skin is made from a fabric that wicks moisture outward, like polypropylene and Capilene. Avoid wearing cotton next to your skin, because it holds rainwater and sweat against your body surface. It is especially critical to keep your head and feet warm, because these are the regions that lose heat the fastest. When you stop to take a rest break, you may need to add a layer of clothing. It also helps to keep your body insulated from cold rocks or gravel that can draw away your body heat.

The key to defeating hypothermia once it starts is to slow heat loss and introduce new heat from an outside source. Warm liquids are a great help, especially if they also contain sugar. A popular folk remedy is to take a nip of booze, but this actually speeds up your heat loss. The alcohol causes the blood vessels at the surface of your skin to expand, and they are soon filled with warm blood from the core of your body. This gives an immediate sensation of warmth, but the blood soon loses its heat to the surrounding air and returns to the body core at a colder temperature. Campfires are rather inefficient at transferring heat, but can be a good way to warm up if the weather is dry and the wood catches fire easily. Portable stoves are much more dependable and efficient: You can warm up one part of your body while the rest is bundled up in insulating layers.

Hypothermia is best stopped in the early stages. Early indications that you might have a problem are uncontrollable shivering and a blue tint to exposed skin. Later, as body temperature is lost, loss of coordination and mental disorientation ensue. If a member of your party begins to show symptoms of hypothermia, get her to a sheltered place and make sure she is dried off, well insulated from the ground, and bundled in warm clothes. Likewise, if you are alone and start experiencing symptoms of hypothermia, you should insulate yourself as well as possible. If you continue to lose heat, you will need an outside heat source such as a stove or hot liquids to warm you up.

7 Making Camp

AFTER a long day of bush-whacking, nothing beats a good hot meal and a warm bed. With a little practice, setting up camp becomes an easy routine that requires little conscious thought. Many aspects of setting up a tight camp are not immediately obvious, however, and it pays to give some special consideration to the fact that you will be camping in spots that are pristine and free from human impacts. Cleared and hardened campsites with fire rings are a rarity in the Alaskan backcountry; this is one of the salient features of untrammeled wilderness. As a result, you will need a little ingenuity in setting up a comfortable camp that does not leave scars on the landscape. This chapter will discuss the basics of setting up a comfortable camp, along with specific information that relates to the special challenges found in the Far North.

The Basics of Campsite Selection

As you grow tired toward the end of the day, it is tempting to plop down at the first flat spot you come across. However, if you are more selective about where you camp, you will have a more comfortable time and avoid many of the pitfalls of sleeping outdoors. It helps to plan ahead by looking at your topo maps to identify likely camping spots. Your primary concerns should be comfort and safety, while convenience should take a back seat. So press on a few more miles, and hold out for that perfect site, because you will be spending a lot of quality time there once you reach it.

One of the primary considerations in selecting a camp spot is the availability of dry, flat ground. If you camp in a marsh, you'll soon be soaked through and the night will likely be long and cold. Similarly, rocky and hummocky ground provides an awfully uncomfortable bed, and one in which you probably won't get much sleep. You should look for a spot with firm, level ground and good drainage. Such spots are commonly found on hilly benches and on bluffs above streams. Look for plants that indicate well-drained soil such as white spruce and grasses. Areas with thick moss provide an added bonus, because the springy moss makes an excellent mattress that molds itself to the shape of your body. Pick a spot that makes a natural mattress as is; mosses are living plants and should never be pulled up to build a bed. Neither should you dig up rocks or otherwise disturb the site in order to get a flat spot to sleep on.

Because most backpackers do not carry enough water to cook with, it will be necessary to set up camp within walking distance of a water source. Beware of camping on the floodplains of streams, however, because heavy rains in the headwaters of the drainage can cause flash flooding. In case of a flash flood, the waters will probably rise faster than you can break camp. If caught in this situation, you stand to lose some of your backpacking gear. Bare gravel is a prime indicator of floodplains, as are willow that have dead vegetation wrapped around the bases of their trunks. Be suspicious of low-lying areas in general, and try to stick to the higher ground for camping. In addition, lakeshores and stream banks are particularly sensitive to disturbance. Camp at least 200 feet away from the nearest surface water. An exception to this rule of thumb are the broad alluvial gravels of the young rivers that weave a braided course down from the high country. Gravel bars are durable camping surfaces, and often contain elevated benches of gravel that are relatively safe from floodwaters.

The unpredictable Alaskan weather can find its way into all but the stoutest tents, so it is wise to choose a campsite that affords some protection from the elements. Tall trees make good windbreaks, as do nearby cliffs and hillsides. Valleys that have frequent bends and twists act as baffles to slow the velocity of the wind, while flat-floored glacial valleys are long and straight and typically turn into wind tunnels during storms. Mountain passes are particularly windy, because the height of the surrounding peaks tends to funnel the wind through the narrow opening of the pass. If you do decide to make camp in a pass, tightly dog down all of your tent flaps against the possibility of high winds. A bit of a breeze can be a blessing, however, if mosquitoes are more of a concern than worsening weather. Mosquitoes are weak fliers, and a 5-mile-per-hour breeze will ground most of them. Look for a spot that is protected from the main wind flow but gets side breezes to keep the insects at bay. If cold weather is anticipated, you should pick a spot that is elevated above the valley floor. Cold air sinks at night, and a low finger ridge might be substantially warmer than a valley-bottom site when morning comes.

In the interest of maintaining your solitude and that of other visitors, it is a good idea to pitch your camp in a spot where it cannot be seen by passing travelers. If there are designated trails in the area, select a spot that is screened from view by trees or shrubs. On the open tundra, side valleys that enter the main river drainages typically offer fine camping spots with the added benefit of seclusion. It is depressing to travel 20 miles into the wilderness only to stumble over someone else's camp. All visitors to the Alaskan backcountry should mask their presence from other parties to ensure that everyone has a quality wilderness experience.

The durability of the site is another prime consideration. In areas that have trails, there may be hardened campsites that have been used repeatedly over the years. If these are present, it is better to use them rather than creating new sites in the environment. In pristine areas, however, sites that appear to have been used once or twice should be avoided so that they can recover their natural character. In such situations, select a site on a well-drained, level surface covered with resistant plants. Sedges and grasses are the most impact-resistant plants, while heather, small shrubs, lichens, and forbs are quite sensitive to trampling. Camp on snow or gravel surfaces that are completely free of vegetation wherever this practice is practical.

One final consideration in selecting a camping spot is to avoid conflicts with the local wildlife. Rodents will chew away on any gear that has food or salt on it, so avoid setting up your camp near vole holes or ground squirrel burrows. To minimize your chances of an unpleasant bear encounter, camp some distance away from obvious travel routes and food sources for wild animals. Game trails should be avoided, as should constricted points in a valley where an animal traveling along will be funneled into a small corridor. Gravel bars are travel corridors for grizzly bears and other wildlife, and travelers who follow these corridors should select a spot that is out of the way to minimize the chance of an unplanned meeting. Remember that most animals follow the easiest path; by climbing up to a bench or rounding a hill you can reduce the chances that a pestiferous critter will invade your camp while you sleep.

Laying Out the Camp

You can often tell experienced backpackers from novices by the tidiness of their camps. Old hands will typically have all of their gear stowed in an appropriate spot where it can be accessed quickly and easily. Neophytes tend to have gear strewn all about the camping area, resting wherever it fell. If you stay organized and avoid tossing gear all over the place, you will reduce the chances of losing important items and at the same time make it more difficult for rodents and other pests to get access to food supplies and sweat-soaked clothing. I like to set up my tent and stow all of my gear immediately upon entering camp, before I do anything else. That way, I have shelter in case a sudden squall blows up, and I never have to set up my tent in the dark.

It is important to set up your tent some distance away from cooking and food storage areas. If possible, locate your cooking site several hundred feet downwind of your tent. That way, if an animal follows the scent of food into your camp, it will not have to walk past the tent to get to the source of the odor. The cooking site and food storage area should also be far apart, so that animals have difficulty getting into your supply of vittles. Once an animal succeeds in breaking into food in a camp, it will associate human camps with the food source and will become a habitual pest.

Securing Your Food

Animals have been raiding camps for food for as long as humans have roamed the planet. In Alaska, tiny log houses on stilts, called caches, were developed to protect the winter food supplies of trappers from voracious wolverines and other beasts. There are a few portable containers that serve as modern equivalents, known broadly as bear-resistant food containers (see Chapter 3). If you don't have one of these containers, you will need to take additional steps to make absolutely certain that animals cannot raid your food supply.

If tall trees are available, you may choose to hang your food from a tall tree limb to further ensure its safety. The food container must hang at least 12 feet above the ground in most cases to be safely out of reach of a standing bear, and at least 20 feet up if the larger coastal brown bears are present in the area. Black bears are able climbers, so make sure that the food is hung at least 6 feet away from the trunk of the tree. You can tie off the other end of the rope to the trunk of a neighboring tree; large boulders are not usually sufficiently secure to serve as anchors for the end of a food line (see Figures 7A and 7B).

If you are caught in a treeless area, you can cache your food under a pile of rocks or atop the ledge of a small cliff. Or, if you are using a drybag to hold your food, you can stow it in underwater as discussed in Chapter 3 (see page 67). In all situations where you cannot hang your food, it is wise to urinate on exposed rocks and trees around your food storage site. It is a proven fact that most mammals are very sensitive to this form of scent marking, and the scent of humans frightens off most wild animals.

FIGURE 7A.

FIGURE 7B. *Bearproof methods for hanging your food.*

Water Supplies

You will need a dependable source of healthy water for drinking and cooking near your camp. In wet tundra, the permafrost keeps water close to the surface of the soil, and seeps and potholes provide suitable water for these purposes. Running water from a nearby stream is even better, because it tends to be less laden with tannins and other chemicals that leach out of decaying vegetation. Glacial streams carry enormous amounts of fine silt suspended in the water column. When using glacial water, you can settle out most of this silt by pouring the water from one pot to another; the heavier sediments remain behind and can be discarded. Do this to avoid getting a dose of grit with your meal. Streams that get their water from snowmelt and groundwater are generally the clearest, except after a rainstorm when they become roiled with sediments. By far the best source of water is a mountain spring, which receives the benefit of having its water naturally filtered by the soil.

Giardia

When you are exerting yourself in the outdoors, your body will have an enormous demand for water. You may pass crystal-clear mountain streams that beckon you to drink deeply and quench your thirst with their cool water. Resist the temptation, because even the most pristine waters may contain Giardia and other aquatic microorganisms and are unsafe for drinking until treated.

Giardia are tiny protozoans that parasitize many wild mammals in Alaska. They cause a condition known as beaver fever because the aquatic habits of the beaver make it a prime vector of the disease. Animals take in the cysts of the organism by drinking affected water, and the tiny Giardia cysts mature and reproduce in the digestive tract. New cysts are shed back into the environment when the infected animal defecates. These cysts survive well in water, and can infect you if you ingest them while drinking from a contaminated water supply.

Tundra with permafrost close to the soil surface is often pocked with small watering holes.

In humans the activities of Giardia in the digestive tract are quite disruptive. The cysts require 10 days to 2 weeks to mature, at which point the victim will begin showing symptoms of the malady. Diarrhea is the most common symptom, and is often accompanied by painful stomach cramps and gas. The medication (called Flagyl) required to treat giardiasis is said by some to be worse than the disease itself, and thus it makes sense to take every precaution to avoid becoming infected.

No water supply can be considered safe, and you must treat all water that could conceivably enter your body. This includes drinking water, water used in cooking, and water used to clean pots and utensils used for eating. The organism can only enter your body orally, so you need not worry about becoming infected by wading through swamps and streams.

There are a number of effective ways to treat water so that Giardia are excluded from it. The most basic way to purify affected water is to bring the water to a full boil for at least a full minute. The heat will kill all of the Giardia, rendering them harmless. A second method that is growing in popularity is to filter the water using equipment specially designed for backpackers. To effectively filter out Giardia, the filter should have a mesh size no larger than 1 micron. These filters are prone to clogging when silty water is used, so if you have one, you would be well advised to avoid glacial streams as water sources. Finally, iodine tablets available at most sporting goods stores are reputed to kill Giardia if used at twice the regular dosage. However, they do not work with full effectiveness in the very cold waters found in Alaska. These tablets also impart a foul taste to the water, and are not recommended for prolonged use.

Snow as a Water Source

When no other water supply is at hand, snow can often be used to fulfill your needs. The water content of snow is actually quite low owing to its crystalline form, with 8 inches of snow equaling about 1 inch of water. Therefore, snow is an inefficient source of water and should not be used if other alternatives are at hand. Snow should not be swallowed directly, because the energetic cost of melting the snow inside your body is quite high and the cold bolus of snow could lower your body core temperature. Snow can be melted in a pot at low temperatures—it helps to put some water in the pot with the melting snow to accelerate the process.

Generally, it is most efficient to seek the downhill side of a snowdrift for source snow. Here, the water trickling downhill from the rest of the melting drift collects to form ice and saturated slush, which has a high water content. Scrape off the top layer of snow, which contains windblown dust (and in some cases, industrial pollutants) to reach the purer stuff underneath.

When using a snowbank as a campsite water source, you can increase your collection efficiency by building a small reservoir. This can be constructed of the mud and dead vegetation at the foot of the snowbank, in the spot where the drainage pattern of the slope appears to converge into a temporary watercourse. During the day, the snow will melt and instead of seeping off down the hill, it will collect in your reservoir, giving you a ready source of water. The reservoir may not be full the next morning, however, because the rate of snowmelt slows during the cooler evening hours.

The Campfire

We humans have been gathering around fires since our cave-dwelling days, and there is something primal and atavistic about staring into the flickering flames and burning embers. Hunters and gatherers used fires for warmth and cooking, built smoky smudges to drive out insects, and deliberately set their environments ablaze to create favorable habitats for game animals. To be sure, the campfire has played an important role in human history.

For the backpacker, however, the campfire is a less than dependable friend. Wood supplies are rather limited in many parts of Alaska, and most tundra areas do not suppport enough woody vegetation to fuel even a tiny blaze. Wet weather frequently renders available material too soggy to carry a flame. In most national parks and wilderness areas, backcountry fires are prohibited to preserve the natural character of the landscape and to minimize human impacts. Thus, the campfire should be looked upon as a luxury item to be enjoyed when the option is available, but not to be depended upon for cooking or warmth. Always carry a portable stove to fulfill these functions.

If you do build campfires during your backcountry explorations, be sure to use minimum-impact techniques to preserve the wild nature of the country. In the past, many authorities have recommended the damaging technique of removing a square of turf from the ground and building a fire within the resulting hole. New studies show that the square of turf almost invariably dies, and this counterproductive method is no longer recommended. Perhaps the best way to have a low-impact campfire is to build a mound fire. This type of fire requires the traveler to bring along a 3-by-3-foot swatch of fireproof cloth or use a flat rock. Gravel is piled on top of the cloth or rock, and the fire is built atop the mound. The gravel insulates the ground from the heat of the fire, preventing damage to the fire site. After the fire is out, the gravel can be emptied back into the original hole from which it was excavated. A logical extension of the mound fire is to dig a pit in streamside gravels and build the fire in it. The remains of the fire are easily buried after it has been extinguished. Do not build a fire ring, which leaves a telltale necklace of scorched stones that betrays your passage and mars the landscape.

Fire Danger

The chances of a campfire igniting a major forest or tundra fire are entirely dependent on the local fire danger. Local Bureau of Land Management and Forest Service offices usually have information on fire danger in public lands. Fire danger is high or extreme after several weeks of hot, dry weather. Arctic and subarctic landscapes usually have plentiful fuel to carry a fire because the rate of decomposition for woody material is so slow in cold climates. Boggy areas, for instance, build up layers of organic peat up to 12 feet deep. If this peat dries out and ignites, it can burn underground for months before emerging as a surface fire. For this reason, you must use the utmost caution when building a campfire to ensure that it doesn't become a deadly and damaging wildfire.

First of all, you should only build campfires when fire danger is low or moderate. Even if your fire is contained in a very small area, sparks blown on the wind can ignite dry duff at some distance from the fire. Second, be certain that your fire is built on mineral soil. Gravel, sand, and rock are good surfaces, but if they are not available, you can carefully remove the topsoil to a depth at which organic matter is no longer present. Subarctic soils are typically thin, and on a dry site you should have little difficulty in removing the organic litter and duff. Finally, be absolutely certain that your fire is out before you retire for the evening. Stir the coals with a stout stick, then douse the fire thoroughly with water until smoke no longer drifts up from the coals. Afterward, test the coals with your bare hand to make sure that there is no warmth emanating from them. This prevents late-night winds from fanning the warm coals into flame. Finally, restore the fire site to its original condition and scatter a little debris over it as camouflage.

Fuel Sources

When gathering wood for a fire, you will need two classes of material: tinder and kindling. Tinder is fine, dry material that ignites readily but does not burn for a long time. Fine twigs make good tinder, as do paper and cardboard. The bark of paper birch is full of flammable resin and makes excellent tinder (use only the bark of dead trees). If no small material is available, you can cut slivers of bark from a dead tree limb. Kindling consists of small to medium-sized branches from 1 to 3 inches in thickness. Kindling sustains the flame ignited in the tinder. In the interest of minimizing the impacts of fire gathering, it is best to use dead and downed wood that you can break up with your hands. These will burn more efficiently and completely than larger logs, and will not leave charred wood behind that is difficult to camouflage.

When searching for kindling, keep an eye out for a variety of different sources. Driftwood that is dry makes excellent firewood, because it has usually had a chance to cure on the beach. Wood found on the ground is often wet and rotten, and will burn slowly, giving off a lot of smoke and little heat. Softwoods, such as spruce and fir, burn hotly and briefly, while hardwoods tend to give off less heat and burn longer. Almost any dry plant part will burn, but the finer ones, such as dry grass and spruce needles, will burn quickly and smother the fire with the ash that they create.

Starting the Fire

It is best to start a fire with a loose pile of tinder with a few very small twigs laid on top. Ignite the pile from the bottom, as flames spread most rapidly in an upward direction. Some people like to use the white gas from their stoves as lighter fluid, but this is a very dangerous practice. White gas is volatile, meaning that it evaporates quickly into a gaseous form. When you pour it onto firewood, it immediately starts to vaporize, and by the time you get a match on it, there is a cloud of gas above the fire itself. This cloud of gas ignites upon lighting, singeing arm hairs and eyebrows and inflicting flash burns on slow-reacting people. It is best to try conventional methods of fire starting first, and then decide whether to risk trying white gas when you cannot get your fire going.

Once you get your fire started, you can begin to add progressively larger pieces of wood. I personally prefer adding on the wood in the shape of a cone or tepee, because this allows the flames to travel easily from the base of the sticks toward the top. More important than the architecture of the fire is maintaining ample air spaces at the base of the fire so that oxygen can reach the flames. If you fail to maintain an adequate passage of air, the fire will smother itself and die. You can use small kindling sticks to carry flame from hot parts of the fire to unlit areas by arranging the kindling diagonally, so that the lower parts of the sticks are in the flames and the upper ends rest against the unlit part of the fire. There is no single fire type that will keep smoke from blowing into your face; if you are lucky, the breeze will be steady and you will be able to avoid the smoke.

Cooking with Fire

Cooking on a campfire is a bothersome and dirty chore, and you are likely to wind up with more than your recommended daily allowance of ash on your food. A fire intended for cooking should be allowed to burn down to coals, which give off more heat than flames and have less of a tendency to blacken pots. Pots and pans can be laid directly on the fire, but I prefer to lay down rocks in the fire itself to serve as tiny legs for my cookware. Items to be baked (such as fish) can be wrapped in aluminum foil and buried in the coals to cook. If you cook with your pots over a wood fire, you will blacken them to some degree. It is best to try to clean the scorched areas as soon as possible. Otherwise, black dust will get all over the inside of your pack as soon as you put your cookware away. One method of preventing this is to coat your pans with soap and pack them in their own plastic bags.

Waste Disposal

Alaska's wilderness remains in its pristine state because the Native peoples who have traveled across it for millenia have trodden lightly. In those few backcountry spots where human activity has made an impact, such as spike camps and mining sites, the landscape is marred by heaps of old garbage. Decomposition occurs at a glacially slow rate in these high latitudes; an orange peel left in the woods for 5 years will still be identifiable. As a result, even the most inconsequential of trash will be around for a long time, spoiling the landscape for those who come after. A special effort must be made by all backcountry visitors to erase all signs of their passage whenever possible.

The disposal of garbage is always problematical when you are backpacking. Some paper and cardboard products may be burned in areas where open fires are allowed. Chances are, however, that not all of your garbage will be combustible, so it is essential to bring along an extra plastic garbage bag to pack out your refuse. This garbage bag should be treated as food from the standpoint of security, and should be kept well out of reach of all marauding animals. If you are fishing, you should dispose of the guts and bones from your fish by puncturing the swim bladder and then tossing the remains far out into the stream or lake from whence they came. This will prevent the smell of fish from drawing scavengers into your camp. Stow garbage in its proper place as soon as it is generated—you would be surprised how little time is required for a gray jay or a ground squirrel to zip in and grab garbage from beneath your nose.

Washing Dishes

Special care must be taken when washing dishes following a meal. Aquatic environments are especially sensitive to tiny amounts of pollution, so every effort must be made to ensure their protection. Commercial dishwashing liquids are deadly to many species of microorganisms, and should be avoided. Special biodegradable detergents are available at backpacking specialty stores; these soaps break down quickly in the environment and are not toxic to aquatic organisms. They do, however, tend to flood the environment with a flush of nutrients above and beyond what is normally available. In order to minimize the impact of this nutrient pulse, you can drain your waste water on the ground away from the stream rather than directly into the water. That way, the soil can act as a filter to remove potentially damaging substances.

There are also several natural alternatives to using soap to wash your dishes. Sand has excellent abrasive qualities, and a handful is enough to provide the grit needed to scour the most recalcitrant grunge. Horsetails, primitive members of the plant kingdom that grow in wet areas, make excellent scouring pads because they are full of silica. If none of these is available, simply scraping your pots with a spoon will get them presentably clean.

Latrine Sites

Relieving yourself in the woods is one of the most peaceful and natural activities around. Cramped, smelly bathrooms with dingy lighting are replaced by sweeping vistas and fresh breezes. Indeed, many find that having a contemplative squat in the wilderness purifies mind, body, and soul. By relieving yourself in the great outdoors, you will be returning important nutrients to the soil, and becoming a part of the great cyclic flow of atoms through the ecosystem. However, you will find few bushes equipped with toilet paper in the backcountry, and some effort will be required to clean up after yourself above and beyond a simple toilet flush.

When preparing to relieve yourself, the first step is to think ahead. You should be downwind of camping and eating areas so that the odor of your bodily wastes is not borne on the wind to any unsuspecting noses. If possible, select a spot of ground that is not underlain by permafrost. On the high tundra, the entire area may be underlain by permafrost that can mummify human waste for years. If this is the case, deposit your waste on the soil surface so that it decomposes more rapidly (for the sake of aesthetics, however, camouflage your efforts). Do not relieve yourself within 200 feet of a stream or standing water, which might easily become contaminated. If you have not brought any commercial toilet paper, plop yourself down near a ready source of natural wiping material.

When you are ready to relieve yourself, prepare the ground by digging a small refuse pit called a cat hole. To minimize your impact on the environment, dig your cat hole beneath a boulder. By doing this, you ensure that you have something with which to cover your pile. Some folks like to hang their rear ends off a log or large boulder. Otherwise, it will be necessary to squat on all fours, crab-style, to accomplish your task. Commercial toilet paper takes years to decompose in Arctic regions; pack out any that you use with the rest of your garbage, rather than burying it with your natural wastes. And in all cases, avoid scented toilet paper because it attracts bears and varmints. Leaves, moss, and snow are good natural substitutes for toilet paper.

Travelers who are planning trips on the Arctic tundra of the high latitudes should consider packing out their solid waste with them. Human waste can be toted cleanly and easily in a short length of PVC tubing that is sealed with screw caps on the ends. Packing out your intestinal creations will keep our Arctic regions from filling up with human droppings, and make for a more pleasant backcountry experience for everyone. It is especially recommended in areas like Denali National Park that get a lot of backpacking use. The practice may one day be required by management agencies.

Breaking Camp

When you leave camp, make an extra sweep through the area to make sure that you have not left anything behind. Take care that anything you brought in is packed away and removed. As a courtesy to those who follow, also pick up any litter left by preceding travelers and pack it out with you. If your passage has swept any part of the soil bare, camouflage the spot by spreading duff or dead leaves over the affected site. If you have built a fire, erase all evidence of it completely. If you have moved small branches away from your tent site, scatter them back onto their original positions. All traces of your visit should be obliterated, so that the site is returned to its original pristine state.

8 Wildlife

WHEN you leave the roads and settlements behind and head out into the bush, you are entering the domain of wild animals that have lived here for millennia. Humans are only passing visitors in these parts, and the true owners of the land are the wild creatures that inhabit it. You must conduct yourself with great respect toward these original inhabitants because Alaska's animals have the ability to seriously impair your expedition if proper precautions are not taken.

Alaska's large mammals have been equipped for survival, and in this harsh land, this includes the ability to defend themselves. Wild animals generally attack people out of fear for their own safety, not because they are naturally violent or savage. Many wild animals will attack a person when they feel threatened, even if the person is not intentionally menacing them. Whether or not you are perceived as a threat by wildlife depends in large measure upon your demeanor.

It is important to communicate your peaceful intentions to animals that you come upon. Direct eye contact is a sign of aggression throughout the animal kingdom, and should be avoided when you find yourself at close quarters with a wild animal. Approaching an animal directly is also looked upon as an intent to attack, whereas backing off and making a quarter turn away from the animal are less threatening responses. Dropping your head below shoulderline for any reason could be construed as an intention to charge, and should also be avoided. Finally, do not make loud noises and quick movements when you find yourself in close proximity with a large animal.

There are some special situations that make encounters between people and wildlife especially dangerous. Most wild animals are genetically programmed to defend their offspring to the death, and thus all animals with youngsters along should be given an especially wide berth. Carnivores defend their kills in a similar manner, and approaching a fresh kill invites attack by the unseen owner. Lastly, animals that are surprised at close quarters may elect to attack if flight does not provide a good alternative. If you can avoid putting yourself in these sorts of situations, you will reduce your chances of a dangerous confrontation.

Bear Encounters

Alaska has three species of bear: the polar bear, the black bear, and the grizzly bear. All are dangerous in their own right, but each has its own set of distinctive traits and each requires a different approach. Many people believe that bears are unpredictable. However, most of their actions can be easily explained, and if you make yourself a student of the body language of bears, you will be able to determine their intentions and hopefully avoid a violent confrontation.

Bears have a simple body language that revolves around threats and displays that communicate their intentions. Threat displays often involve standing broadside to the intended audience as a display of the bear's bulk. An elevated form of threat involves swinging the massive head from side to side and snapping the teeth loudly. These two threats are designed to cow the opponent, and do not communicate an intent to attack. If a bear lowers its head and tucks it between its front paws, though, look out! This is the intention to charge, and will be followed shortly by a rush. Most charges are false ones; in almost all cases, the bear will stop charging short of its target to display again.

Most wild bears are afraid of humans, and will move off as soon as they sense your presence. In fact, because it is better attuned to its environment than you are, a bear will often sense your presence and move away before you even know that it was there. The most dangerous bears are the ones that have lost their natural fear of humans through a process called habituation. In this process, a bear that succeeds in stealing garbage or food from a cabin or campsite comes to associate the smell of humans with food. Such a bear looks upon encampments as possible food sources, and because the smell of humans is now familiar, the bear will not flee when approached by people. Habituated bears will be problem bears for life, and the only way to remedy the situation is to have the bear destroyed or to remove it to an uninhabited area from which it can never return. Relocation efforts are seldom successful and usually result in the death of the animal.

Polar Bears. The polar bear is a maritime mammal, living for most of the year on the sea ice that covers the Arctic Ocean. During lean winters, polar bears wander into northern coastal communities to scavenge and hunt. Humans are looked upon by hungry polar bears as easy meals, and are hunted actively even in populated areas. However, polar bears will stick to the sea ice during most winters, and rarely pose a threat even to coastal villages in the Far North. During the summer, these bears are typically absent from the land, and pose no danger whatsoever to summer visitors.

Black Bears. Black bears are the smaller cousins of grizzlies and polar bears, although under ideal conditions they may attain weights of well over 300 pounds. They do not thrive where grizzly and brown bears are present, and are generally abundant only where these larger bears are few or absent. Black bears often manifest themselves as campground pests, rummaging through garbage cans and unprotected coolers. Occasionally, large black bears will hunt humans for meat. No one knows why they do this because such circumstances are highly unusual. However, it seems that black bears find human flesh to be quite edible, and the occasional rogue black bear that kills a person is likely to eat its victim.

Most experts agree that the best approach to dealing with a smaller black bear is to act aggressively and chase it out of the area. Larger bruins should be backed away from slowly. Female black bears with cubs seek only to protect their young; give them a wide berth as well. Black bears can climb trees with ease, so taking to the trees in hopes of escaping them is a poor strategy. If you are attacked, you should defend yourself vigorously, beating on the bear with any available weapon until the bear gives up. If you play dead, you will merely become an easy meal.

Grizzly Bears. The grizzly bear is the most fearsome peril that you are likely to face in the Alaskan backcountry. This bear is present throughout most of the state in one form or another, and because it is so common, it poses the greatest threat to backpackers. Along the coast, a salmon-eating variety known as the Alaskan brown bear or Kodiak bear inhabits river valleys. These large bears may exceed 1000 pounds in weight and stand over 9 feet tall on their hind legs. The smaller grizzly bear of the interior averages only about 300 pounds at adulthood, and is characterized by a concave face, pronounced shoulder hump, and silver-tipped fur (see Figure 8). The interior grizzly is much more aggressive than its larger coastal cousin, and is more likely to attack humans.

Grizzly bears will not eat human meat unless they are starving; a grizzly that kills a person will generally abandon its kill in search of a more savory meal. Grizzlies attack because they feel threatened, and thus it is important when encountering a grizzly to behave in a manner that is reassuring to the bear. To avoid unpleasant confrontations, make noise as you move through habitats with poor visibility, so that animals ahead of you can hear your approach and move off to a safe distance.

If you see a bear, your best strategy for avoidance depends on the bear's disposition toward you. If you see the bear in the distance and it is unaware of your presence, you should adjust your route to pass as far away from the bear as possible. Avoid

FIGURE 8.

making any noise that might give away your presence. If a bear in the distance sees you as well, it is wise to wave your arms slowly above your head and call out to the bear so that it can identify you as a human. If the bear is quite close to you and still does not sense your presence, try to back away slowly and quietly to avoid disturbing it. Bears that you encounter at close range must be handled with extreme caution.

Let the natural capabilities and shortcomings of the bear dictate your retreat. Grizzly bears cannot climb trees because their claws are too long. You can take refuge in a tree until the bear moves on if (and only if) you can find a tree that you can climb before the bear can drag you out of it. Unfortunately, most of the trees in Alaska are too small and/or difficult to climb to afford a good refuge. There is a pervasive myth that grizzly bears cannot run downhill. Not only can they do so, but they can also do it a lot faster than you can, so running downhill is a poor strategy. In fact, running in any capacity is a poor bet, because it will only cause the bear to think that you are an escaping prey item. This triggers the bear's natural instinct to give chase. Bears have a top speed of 40 miles per hour, so a running man doesn't even stand a chance of escaping. The bear will ultimately decide that a fleeing person is inedible, but only after the person has been subdued.

Should you find yourself face to face with a grizzly bear, you will need to control the situation through body language and posturing. Back away slowly, waving your arms gently above your head. In my encounters with bears, I have found that it helps to talk to the bear in low, soft tones. By "reasoning" with the bear ("I'm not very good to eat; not much fat here; probably wouldn't even make one meal," and so on), you can steady your own nerves and at the same time serve notice to the bear that you pose no threat. When you are out of sight and a safe distance away, you can start making tracks in the other direction. Even then, however, walk quickly and do not run.

If the bear charges you, remain still and let it come. Chances are good that the charge is a false one and the bear will pull up short before it reaches you. If you run at this point, you face almost certain injury. If the bear does not stop its rush and does move in to maul you, curl up in the fetal position and play dead. Draw your knees up to your chest to protect your vital organs, and lock your hands behind your neck to protect it from a bite. The grizzly is a powerful opponent that you will not be able to overcome. If you continue to struggle against the bear, it will certainly maul you thoroughly. By playing dead, you attempt to satisfy the bear that you are no longer a threat, and it should leave you alone with relatively minor wounds.

Many Alaskans tote handguns into the backwoods to fend off attacking grizzlies. This is unwise for several reasons. First of all, with a handgun comes a false sense of security. People who carry handguns feel safe, and often do not take the necessary precautions to avoid an encounter entirely. By contrast, hikers who enter the woods weaponless are acutely aware of their perilous position, and will take appropriate measures to ensure their own safety. Secondly, grizzly bears are difficult to kill with mere handgun bullets. The grizzly has a thick skull plate that can turn a bullet, and its other vital organs are hidden in a mass of flesh that makes it an uncertain target. Not only must you hit the bear in the vitals, but also you must stop the bear dead in its tracks to prevent it from mauling you before it finally dies. This is an unlikely proposition at best, and thus handguns make a poor defense against bears. If you feel the need to carry a firearm into the woods, carry a shotgun armed with lead slugs. This weapon is only effective at short range, but has the stopping power that pistols lack.

There are also commercially available bear repellents that shoot a fine mist of cayenne pepper into the eyes, nose, and mouth of a bear. This blinds the bear temporarily, allowing the hiker to make an escape. However, these sprays do not work well in strong winds. A biologist acquaintance of mine recently had the opportunity to test bear spray during a summer field-season in Denali National Park. A grizzly approached the biologist and his assistant repeatedly, and finally the biologist pulled out his bear spray and sprayed it at the approaching bear. The wind blew all of the pepper away from the bear's face, but the sound of the spray leaving the can was sufficient to scare off the offending animal. Tests in controlled conditions do suggest that the spray is effective in turning away even enraged bears if it hits them squarely in the face.

Moose Encounters

Moose are present throughout Alaska, and their favorite haunts are typically brushy areas that bring moose and unwary hikers together at close quarters. The danger with moose is the possibility of being trampled beneath the powerful hooves. Rutting bulls may also use their antlers on a perceived threat, but during most of the summer the antlers are in velvet and are much too tender to be used as weapons. Big bulls may weigh as much as 1300 pounds, and cow moose typically reach an adult weight of around 800 pounds. Cows with calves are particularly foul tempered, and should be given a wide berth. However, moose act instinctively and are fairly predictable in their behavior.

If you read it properly, moose body language will communicate all you need to know to avoid a conflict. When a moose first perceives your presence, it will stop what it is doing and stare intently at you with its ears cocked forward, straining to determine what manner of creature you are. This is not an aggressive posture, but merely an inquisitive one. You can back off at this point without provoking an attack. If the moose drops its ears straight down or gives you a sideward glance with rolling eyes, it is expressing displeasure at your presence, and it is best to beat a hasty retreat. If the moose drops its head below shoulderline while its ears are dropped, it is preparing to charge, and you had better start running.

Unlike bears, moose interpet running as a sign that you are not a threat to it. Moose defend themselves against predators by standing at bay; indeed, a moose that is able to turn and face its attackers is almost guaranteed to escape the encounter unharmed. A predator that is forced to turn tail and flee from a moose is no longer a threat, and thus most moose charges are designed to cause the attacker to flee. Very rarely do moose complete their charge and actually attack; almost all charges are brought up short of the target. Thus, when you are charged by an angry moose, all you need to do is to run away to satisfy the moose's need for security.

Campsite Pests

Rodents. While backpacking, you must always be aware that your pack and clothing may become targets for raiding animals. Not only will rodents seek to eat unguarded lunches, but they will also chew pack straps and hip belts for salt. Salt is rare in high Arctic ecosystems, and is thus a highly valued commodity for wild animals. If you stop to rest near a ground squirrel burrow or a series of vole tunnels, you can expect these little critters to make the most of the dietary supplements that you carry with you into the wilds. To avoid mishaps of this sort, check a rest area for signs of rodent activity before you stop, and keep a watchful eye on your pack and clothing while they are in a place accessible to small animals.

Campsite Scavengers. There are a number of birds and mammals that make raids on unattended campsites. Coastal sea gulls will attack food that is left out in the open, and so will their inland counterpart, the gray jay. Ravens are present throughout Alaska, and are skilled camp robbers. These large birds have their own complex language, learn quickly, and team up together on cooperative ventures. They are so intelligent that they frequently appear in Alaska Native legends as tricksters. Along the coast, raccoons may be a problem. Most folks don't generally think of these furry creatures as Alaskan animals, but they inhabit the coastal archipelagoes of southeast Alaska and can be quite cunning in obtaining hidden food.

Insects. Alaska is renowned for its bounty of winged avengers that attempt to draw the lifeblood from any approaching warm-blooded creature. On the coastal plain of the Arctic Ocean, mosquitoes and botflies reach densities sufficient to drive caribou herds into snowy areas that lack good forage. These buzzing hordes can prove a real mortal threat to warm-blooded animals; some caribou have been killed from sheer loss of blood by especially dense swarms of insects. These biting insects can prove to be more than a match for hikers as well, as explorer Addison Powell attested in the account of his Alaskan travels: "The mosquitoes had caused us fully to realize the mistake that had been made when we were born; but they now left us, and the gnats took their places until our ears attained the thickness of ordinary boot-soles." Indeed, many Alaskans hail the mosquito as the state bird.

The severity of insect pests depends largely on season, temperature, and local topographic features. In general, most insect pests are grounded by temperatures much cooler than 50 degrees Fahrenheit because their wing muscles are not warm enough to allow flight. Periodic freezes may even kill entire mosquito and gnat populations, and this fact accounts for the relative scarcity of insects in early spring and late summer. Warm temperatures are ideal flying weather for most insects, and hot, windless days often produce the worst bug swarms.

With the exception of biting flies, the biting insects in Alaska are weak flyers, and have a hard time in moderate to strong winds. It is often wise to seek relief on a windy ridgeline when biting insects are especially numerous.

Low, swampy areas typically harbor the highest densities of insect pests. Mosquitoes and some gnats have aquatic larvae that depend on standing water to develop into biting adults. If you plan to venture into boggy areas during midsummer, you would be well advised to bring a head net with you to prevent these pestiferous aviators from driving you completely out of your mind. Conversely, higher, well-drained ground is often relatively bug-free, providing a welcome respite from the buzzing hordes of the low country.

Today's insect repellents are quite advanced, and some offer complete protection from marauding insects. The most effective chemical in this regard is Diethyl-metatoluamide (DEET); it is found in most commercial insect repellents in varying levels of strength. Some repellents boast 100 percent DEET, and will make you well-nigh bug-proof. However, these super-strength versions are corrosive enough to melt plastic, and have an unpleasant oily feel to them. In addition, these chemicals have been linked to liver problems, and thus should be used as sparingly as possible. Weaker dosages mixed in with moisturizing lotions are probably better for your skin. Skin-So-Soft, a commercial beauty lotion, also has good insect repellent qualities, and is ideal for hikers who are concerned about their complexions.

Wildlife Viewing

Alaska is home to some of the last undisturbed ecosystems in the world. The presence of humans in this remote landscape has been a relatively recent occurrence; the first people crossed the Bering Land Bridge from Siberia to Alaska only about 27,000 years ago. The harsh weather and short growing seasons kept human populations in Alaska at low levels in the past, and such populations did little to disturb the natural cycles of their ecosystems. But modern technology is now allowing a population boom in the 49th state, and industrial development is beginning to put pressure on Alaska's natural systems in the state. However, most of Alaska is unsuited for farming and logging, and it has thus far escaped the ravages of intensive land use that characterize the lower 48 states.

Alaska provides opportunities for viewing wild animals in their natural habitats that rival those found on the savannah parklands of Africa. Broad expanses of open tundra, boreal forests, and diverse coastal ecosystems are within easy reach of the road system. Caribou run free in great herds, migrating in groups of hundreds of thousands across miles of untouched, primeval landscape. The grizzly bear still occupies the top position in the food chain, and occasional bear attacks remind the smug that humans do not always have the last word in these parts. In many areas, Alaskan wildlife shows little or no fear of humans, who consequently are treated to the unique thrill of viewing some of nature's most magnificent beasts up close in their natural habitats. With this privilege comes responsibility, however; wild animals can always be dangerous and must be treated with the utmost respect. By learning the habits and characteristics of the various kinds of Alaskan wildlife, you can enter their domain confident in your ability to avoid harm to yourself and the natural inhabitants alike.

When viewing wildlife, your first concern should be the welfare of the animals that you are observing. Many people believe that wildlife viewing is a nonconsumptive use of the environment, but in many cases this is not so. In the name of curiosity, lots of folks engage in behavior that creates stress for the wildlife they are observing. Scaring an incubating duck off its nest or spooking a caribou with its calf might have dire short- and long-term consequences for the young. Inquire locally to find out times and habitats that are critical to wildlife, such as nesting and calving areas and seasons, and do not approach animals when they are in such vulnerable circumstances. If your actions might possibly be disturbing the subject animals, stop what you are doing and move away until you are no longer agitating them.

A good rule of thumb is to watch animals only in such a way that your presence does not provoke a change in their behavior. Most animals have an invisible comfort zone around them; they will not allow any threatening animal (including humans) to approach within this zone. Respect the comfort zone of the animals that you are watching, and you will be rewarded with a privileged glimpse into their innermost secrets. Watch animals closely for signs of uneasiness, and back away if your presence becomes a disruption to their activities.

Wild animals should be approached silently from a downwind direction. Avoid sudden movements, and never pursue an animal that is moving away. A spotting scope or binoculars will allow you to get a closer look without spooking the animals that you are watching. Wild animals are typically most tolerant of human presence in areas where they are protected from hunting.

Above all, never allow wild animals to obtain human food for any reason. Animals have been attuned to a rigorous diet of wild foods by thousands of years of natural selection, and feeding them always has damaging results. The foreign chemical composition and associated microbes found in human food are likely to cause digestive problems in a wild animal. In cases where this is not so, the feeding of wild animals transforms them into beggars that haunt campgrounds and rest areas. Such scavengers often lose their ability to forage for themselves in their natural habitats, and are unable to survive the rigors of the landscape when their human patrons disappear.

Caribou. The barren-ground caribou found in Alaska inhabit tundra and open boreal forest in the northern two-thirds of the state. Caribou eat sedges and the tender shoots of shrubs during the summer, while lichens are the preferred winter food. These animals are quite social throughout the year, and form huge calving herds during the late spring. In some areas, caribou herds undertake migrations that span thousands of miles as they move from sheltered winter ranges to high Arctic calving grounds. At the time this book was written, certain caribou populations that are easily accessible were declining in response to the combined effects of poor range conditions, heavy hunter harvests, a series of hard winters, and wolf predation.

Caribou are generally quite skittish around people, and are best viewed from a distance. If you approach them too closely, they will flee long distances to escape. If you wish to get into close proximity with a group of caribou, your best bet is to figure out which direction the animals are headed, and sit down quietly in their path. Because caribou require several signs (like a quick movement or a suspicious scent) to identify danger, they will generally ignore you as long as you remain perfectly still. This method of approaching caribou is also favored by local hunters.

Look for caribou in open expanses of grassland or tundra near or above the timberline. Caribou are most typically seen on high, well-drained ground, and tend to avoid swampy areas. Forests with little underbrush and widely scattered trees may also harbor these elusive beasts, but they are difficult to view in this setting.

Caribou often use river bars as travel corridors.

The Porcupine herd is perhaps the most famous herd of caribou in the world, and has been featured in numerous television programs and books. This herd winters in the Ogilvie Mountains, and migrates north through the Brooks Range to its summer calving grounds in the Arctic National Wildlife Refuge and a neighboring Canadian preserve. The Western Arctic herd is the largest, having over 500,000 animals. It roams the mountains and tundra north of Kotzebue. The Central Arctic herd is perhaps a splinter group of the Western Arctic herd, and is often sighted near Prudhoe Bay. The Denali herd summers in Denali National Park and winters on the Tanana lowlands. It is protected from hunting on its summer range, and here it can be viewed with ease. The Delta herd makes its home along the northeastern flanks of the Alaska Range. The Nelchina herd inhabits the Copper River Basin, and motorists sometimes spot parts of it from the Denali Highway. The Mentasta herd roams the northern part of Wrangell–St. Elias National Park and the neighboring Bureau of Land Management lands, and the Fortymile herd inhabits the rolling uplands near Eagle, Alaska.

Muskox. This shaggy, sheep-sized creature is native to the open tundra of the high Arctic. During the 19th century, Alaskan muskox populations were completely wiped out by commercial whalers and sealers. These stout tundra dwellers were reintroduced from Greenland in the 1950s, and now there are several healthy populations in the state. The largest population is on Nunivak Island, in the Bering Strait, and there is also a rapidly expanding population on the Seward Peninsula. There are several small but growing herds in the Sadlerochit River area of the Arctic National Wildlife Refuge. This population has been dispersing westward for some time, and they are occasionally spotted in the Franklin Bluffs area by travelers along the Dalton Highway. Muskox are raised commercially for their fine underfur, called *quiviut,* which is used to make knitted products. There is a commercial farm near Palmer (northeast of Anchorage) that offers public tours. Travelers can also view captive muskox at the University of Alaska experimental farm outside of Fairbanks.

Moose. Moose are distributed widely throughout Alaska, and indeed are a primary food staple in bush communities throughout the state. Alaskan moose are a distinct subspecies that contrast with their North American cousins in a number of ways. Alaskan moose form social groups, and during the autumn they breed in rutting harems that may exceed 40 animals. These moose are adapted to the open environment of treelines and open forest, and have a light-colored pelage on their backs that helps them blend in with the shrubs. Alaskan moose are browsers, and their primary forage is composed of young twigs from willow and other shrubs. They will also eat aquatic plants in places where these delicacies are available. The largest moose in the world come from the Alaska Peninsula in the southwestern corner of the state.

These two bull moose got their antlers locked together while fighting for dominance during the fall rut. They may have died of starvation, or perhaps a predator made an easy meal of them.

The Alaskan moose is so imposing that few predators even try to tackle adult animals. Some of the wolves autopsied by the Alaska Department of Fish and Game had over 20 broken bones that had healed over, presumably broken in attempts to bring down this dangerous animal. One study in the Brooks Range found that wolves continued to actively hunt caribou even when moose were abundant and caribou were scarce. Moose cows regularly take on adult grizzly bears in defense of their calves. Cow moose typically outweigh interior grizzlies by 500 pounds, and are often successful in driving the bears away. Both grizzlies and wolves take a fair number of moose calves each year, and may also take adult bulls that have been exhausted or injured during the fall rut.

Moose are rarely seen in large numbers, but their abundance in a broad variety of lowland habitats makes them a dependable attraction for wildlife enthusiasts. Moose can be found in wet lowlands and near the treeline, where the luxuriant growth of bushes supports their hearty appetite. It is best to enjoy moose from a respectful distance, as they can be aggressive when threatened. One of the best places to look for moose is the Kenai National Wildlife Refuge. This area was set aside by President Franklin D. Roosevelt to be managed as a moose range. The eastern side of Denali National Park and the neighboring lowlands near Cantwell are also good places to spot moose. There are a few all-white moose (they are not albinos) in the population that roams the northern edge of the Alaska Range.

Dall Sheep. These pure white relatives of the bighorn sheep flourish in alpine environments in all parts of the state except the southeastern panhandle. They feed together in social bands, usually with the rams separated from the females and young. They feed on grasses and forbs in alpine meadows, never straying far from the steep terrain that affords them protection from predators. On cliffs, Dall sheep are incredibly nimble, and can run at full speed across rock faces that would be impassable to climbers without ropes. Breeding season is in

Dall sheep segregate into single-sex herds during the summer. Here, a band of ewes and lambs grazes on the mountain tundra of Denali National Park.

November, and the rams engage in lengthy head-butting contests to determine which rams will get to participate in the breeding activities.

Dall sheep are quite approachable, especially in areas where they are not hunted. In general, sneaking behavior tends to spook these animals to a greater degree than a slow, direct approach. In addition, always approach them from below and avoid cutting them off from the steep slopes that form their escape route. Sheep are quite sensitive to animals (including humans) that approach from above. Because Dall sheep inhabit areas that have little visual cover, their antics are easy to observe. Bring along a pair of binoculars for the most revealing look into their world, because they frequently inhabit forbidding terrain that prevents a close approach.

The best place to view Dall sheep is on the lower mountains of Denali National Park; Kluane National Park in the Yukon is also a good bet. There are also healthy populations in the Wrangell Mountains, Chugach State Park, and the Brooks

Range. At least some parts of these latter herds are hunted, and you may have to hike deep into the mountains to find them. The best time to view them is during late summer, when the snows have left the lower slopes. Do not disturb them during the lambing season, which runs into mid-June.

Mountain Goats. These hardy mountain creatures occur throughout southeastern Alaska, ranging north as far as the Talkeetna Mountains to the north of Anchorage. They are quite shy and limited to steep country, so they are rarely seen in large numbers. Their shaggy white coats make them difficult to distinguish from the patches of snow that dot their environment. You will need a spotting scope or binoculars if you want to view these elusive beasts, as they will rarely tolerate the presence of humans close by. Kenai Fjords National Park and Glacier Bay National Park are both good places to look for these cliff-hanging mammals.

Wolves. These social hunters are thinly dispersed across the length and breadth of the state, but owing to the large size of each pack's territory, wolves are rarely seen by humans. Wolves actively avoid human contact, and healthy wolves pose absolutely no threat to backcountry visitors. The best habitat for wolf viewing is open tundra, where these magnificent animals can be seen at great distances; Denali National Park and the north slope of the Brooks Range are the best places to look for them.

Wolves occur in social groups, called packs, that travel and hunt together. The pack is organized around a dominant pair of animals that are the only animals allowed to breed. During the spring denning season, all members of the pack work together to provide food for the growing pups, who cannot venture far from the safety of the den. The packs may disband during late fall, when food becomes scarce. These packs are highly territorial, and mark their boundaries with urine and feces just like domestic dogs. From time to time, you may hear wolves howling to each other across great distances. This howling serves to cement the social bonds among pack members and to advertise ownership of the territory to neighboring packs.

Wolves are specialists at running down large animals, but will actively hunt smaller ones when the opportunity arises. They have incredible stamina, and will chase their prey for miles until the prey animal falters or the wolves become exhausted. They preferentially target weak and sick animals because they are easier to catch. Caribou are their favorite food, and they will also take Dall sheep when the sheep venture too far from the safety of the cliffs. Moose are a dangerous prey, and for the most part wolves will only try to capture calves and weakened adults. There is some evidence that each wolf in the pack may have a specific role in making the kill. One wolf may grab the prey by the nose and weigh it down, while a second goes for the rear haunch or the neck area. Packs may specialize in certain prey types as well. One study found that when the dominant wolves in one pack were killed, the remaining wolves were was no longer able to capture moose as they had done before.

Bears. The best place from which to view bears is the inside of your car. A respectful distance of at least a quarter mile should always be maintained when watching bears, and under no circumstances should they be approached. These animals will not tolerate the close proximity of humans, and may attack if they feel threatened. Black bears are most common in southeast and south-central Alaska, while grizzly bears dominate the interior and northern regions. The McNeill River sanctuary provides guided viewing of giant brown bears up close in a controlled environment to the lucky few who draw permits to visit each year. Visitors to Denali National Park can usually count on seeing a few grizzlies along the park road. Grizzlies are actively hunted throughout most of the state, and are likely to be skittish outside the boundaries of national parks.

In spring, grizzly bears can be found on open tundra and river bars, living on a diet of peavine roots and ground squirrels, along with the occasional scavenged carcass. They graze throughout the summer on tundra benches, and may occasionally be fortunate enough to catch a calf moose or caribou to supplement their diet. They switch their food-gathering efforts to abundant wild berries beginning in mid-August, and this source provides the largest portion of their diet until they enter their dormant winter denning period. Grizzly bears enter a deep sleep that lasts through the long winter months, and pregnant sows give birth to their young during this time.

Small Carnivores. Red foxes abound throughout most of Alaska, inhabiting boreal forests where they live on a diet of snowshoe hares and small rodents. Arctic foxes, their short-legged cousins to the north, make their living hunting lemmings and voles on the open tundra. These small and inquisitive predators have a dark pelage that turns white during the winter. Coyotes are present as far north as Denali National Park, and are quite common on the Kenai Peninsula. Lynx represent the only members of the cat family to inhabit Alaska, and are confined to forested areas, where they are rarely seen. The largest populations are on the Kenai Peninsula and in interior Alaska. Lynx numbers are closely linked with the cyclical population fluctuations of their main prey, the snowshoe hare. Likewise, pine martens and weasels abound in forested areas, but are seen only occasionally. Mink and river otters inhabit streamside habitats in southeast and south-central Alaska, while sea otters are commonly spotted playing in the coastal waters of southeast and south-central Alaska.

Beaver. These aquatic mammals inhabit streams and lakes throughout the state. Their diet of tree bark and twigs limits them to areas with abundant hardwoods, where they slave away throughout the summer, cutting down trees that will furnish their winter food supply. Beaver live in large lodges constructed of sticks and mud, with underwater entrances that prevent predators from gaining access. Beaver on streams and rivers build elaborate dams that raise the water level above the level of the lodge entrance. In the process, they create habitat for trout and grayling. Beaver have webbed feet that help them propel themselves through the water, and their broad, flat tails can be brought down onto the water's surface with a loud slap to warn their fellows when danger is approaching. In winter, a beaver clan never emerges above the ice of the pond, remaining within the warmth and safety of the lodge where the young are born.

Other Small Animals. Alaska is home to a diverse host of rodents and lagomorphs that can provide hours of viewing enjoyment to the interested observer. In mountainous areas, several species of marmot, a woodchuck-sized rodent, inhabit fields of loose boulders. The most commonly sighted species is the hoary marmot, which inhabits mountains from the Alaska Range southward. The Brooks Range has its own species of marmot, called the Alaska marmot, which has close relatives in Siberia. The pika, a small, short-eared relative of the rabbit, also inhabits talus slopes. This shy creature is known for its piercing alarm whistle, which seems to come from everywhere and nowhere. Arctic ground squirrels live colonially in grassy tundra areas, and can be quite comical in their antics. Both the collared lemming of the Far North and the snowshoe hare shed their dull brown pelage for a coat of pure white that camouflages them from predators during the winter months. Each of these two animals experiences a cyclical population boom every 11 years.

Birds. Alaska is home to a diverse assemblage of birds that extends to the tallest peaks and the most northerly latitudes. Most of these birds are summer residents and disappear during the long Alaskan winters. Among the permanent residents are the raven, the gray jay, and, in southeast Alaska, the water ouzel. I will only discuss a few of the more interesting varieties here; complete guides to the birds of Alaska can be found at most bookstores.

In southeastern and south-central Alaska, the bird fauna is dominated by marine birds. Huge rookeries of seagoing kittiwakes, murres, puffins, and gulls cluster on tiny offshore islands. The majestic bald eagle plies its trade along the coast and its river systems, following salmon runs in search of an easy meal. Farther north, the golden eagle makes its home among mountain crags, and its cries can be heard throughout alpine areas. The pothole lakes of the interior and the North Slope are dotted with waterfowl nesting grounds, which feature such spectacular birds as the trumpeter swan and several species of goose. The willow ptarmigan, a grouse-sized ground nester, is the official state bird. It remains in Alaska all year, donning white plumage for the winter, when it subsists on a diet of willow buds and frozen berries.

Interpreting Animal Signs

Your ability to spot animals in their native habitats will be greatly enhanced if you can identify other signs that indicate wildlife activity. Tracks, bones, rubs, and dung piles all tell stories about the animals that left them behind. These are subtle clues to the daily rhythms of wildlife activity, and to find them, you will have to keep a sharp eye on your surroundings. By doing so, you will find that you become more attuned to the environment that you are moving through, and thus will get more out of your wilderness experience.

Tracks

Tracks left by passing animals are some of the more common signs you will find during the course of your travels. Your ability to find tracks is largely dependent on the density of wild animals in the area and the ability of the ground to retain the foot impressions of the animal in question. Silty mud and snow make excellent tracking surfaces, while hard, rocky ground and grassy meadows make tracking a real challenge.

The age of the tracks can be determined to some extent by the sharpness of their outline; fresh tracks will be sharp all around the edges, but will begin to crumble and blur with the passage of time. During dry spells, track sets can be preserved

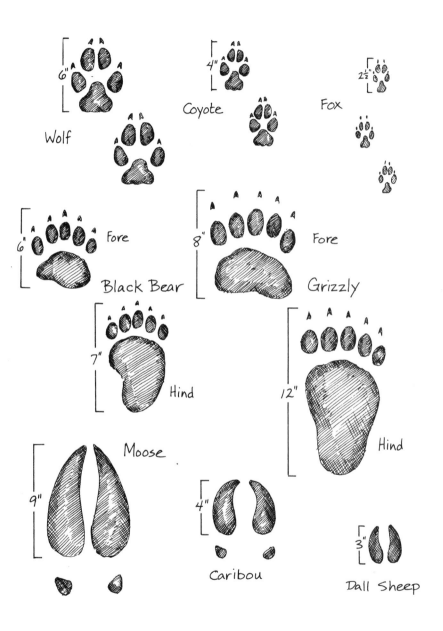

Wolf

Coyote

Fox

Black Bear   Fore

Grizzly   Fore

Black Bear   Hind

Grizzly   Hind

Moose

Caribou

Dall Sheep

FIGURE 9. *Tracks of some common Alaskan mammals*

for long periods of time, while rainstorms usually erase tracks quite quickly. By figuring out the age of a track, you can determine roughly how long it has been since its maker passed that way.

Large herbivores walk on their toenails, and only leave impressions of this part of their feet. The twin half-moons of most herbivore prints represent the two toenails that together form a cloven hoof. The identity of the track's owner can often be inferred from the habitat in which it is found. For instance, smaller tracks found on a steep scree slope usually belong to Dall sheep or mountain goats. The two tracks most often confused are those of caribou and moose. The tracks of moose are longer (averaging about 9 inches in length compared to 6 inches for caribou), and have a more tapered appearance.

In addition to the two main toes, large herbivores have two vestigial toes, complete with tiny toenails, that are found higher up on the leg of the animal. These vestigial toes, called dew claws or "cloots," may come into contact with the ground when the animal is on soft ground or is running, leaving two tiny impressions behind each hoof print. When alarmed, members of the deer family, most particularly caribou, splay their hooves apart widely as they run, leaving a characteristic track.

Large carnivores walk on their toes and the balls of their feet, leaving tracks that represent the foot pad and array of toes in front of it. Members of the dog family tend to have tracks that are longer than they are wide, while cats leave tracks that are round or are wider than they are long. In addition, members of the dog family, including wolves and foxes, leave tiny claw marks with their footprints, whereas cats have retractable claws and thus do not leave claw prints. Within the dog family, track size is the best clue when determining the type of animal that made the track. Wolves have the largest tracks (4 to 5 inches), while coyotes have middle-sized tracks (2¾ inches) and foxes leave the smallest prints (2¼ inches). It is difficult to differentiate the tracks of domestic dogs from those of their wild relatives, but this problem is only acute in areas immediately next to human settlements. The lynx is the only wild member of the cat family in Alaska, and thus can be identified quickly and easily by its round, four-toed print that lacks claw marks.

Bears walk on the balls of their front feet, and use the entire foot for support in the rear. Thus, the print of the hind foot has a long pad, making the tracks easy to identify. In general the tracks of grizzly bears are larger than those of black bears, although there is some overlap between immature grizzlies and large adult black bears. The grizzly bear has much longer claws, however, and these claws leave their mark from 4 to 8 inches in front of the toepads. Black bears, in contrast, have much shorter claws that leave their impressions only an inch or two in front of the toes. Coastal brown bears leave the largest tracks of all, and the forefoot of a mature animal may leave tracks that are more than a foot in diameter.

The tracks of smaller animals are much more difficult to tell apart; many rodents possess tracks that are almost identical to those of small carnivores. However, one smaller animal, the snowshoe hare, does have distinctive tracks. As it bounds along, the front legs land on the ground first, making two small, round prints. The hare then extends its hind legs *in front of* the forefeet before it plants them, leaving two long prints just forward of the prints of the forefeet. These tracks are seen most commonly in winter, when snow blankets the forest habitats of hares and renders their tracks easy to identify.

It is difficult to track down an animal in order to find it. Animals generally move through their habitats more rapidly than you will, due to their superior familiarity with the terrain. In addition, tracks along the animals' route may appear for a time only to disappear as the animals travel across grassy or hard surfaces. Finally, most animals are very wary of approaching predators, and watch their back trail to prevent surprise attacks. Tracks are by far most useful as an index to the density of animals in a given habitat, and the presence of animals at one spot during the past makes it more likely that there will be animals of the same type lurking nearby during the present.

Scat

During the course of your travels, you will inevitably come across dung piles left by the animals native to the area you are exploring. Most scat piles are fairly east to identify, and thus can give you additional clues to the lives of the native inhabitants. Indeed, biologists sometimes use the density of scat piles in an area as an index to the concentration of critters using the site. You need not wade into the filth to identify its maker; visual identification can be made easily from a distance of a few feet.

Herbivores leave telltale pellet groups that result from their fibrous diets. In the large intestine, these herbivores withdraw almost all of the water from their feces, and the round, dry pellets that emerge are the result of this conservation of water. Moose leave the largest pellets, averaging about 1 inch in length and round to oval in shape. Beware of the person who offers you chocolate-covered almonds in Alaska! The pellets of other herbivores are much more difficult to tell apart. Deer, caribou, and Dall sheep have round pellets that are about ¼ inch in diameter. To tell them apart, evaluate the habitat in which they were found. Remember that caribou and Dall sheep overlap quite a bit in their habitat selection. Look for tracks in conjunction with the pellets to determine which herbivore left the scat.

Bears generally leave large, formless piles of logs, each of which can be up to 3 inches in diameter. Because the diet of bears is quite variable, the scats also vary. If the bear has been eating a lot of meat, the scats will be dark brown to black. In berry season, bear scats take the form of liquid pies, rich in entire, undigested berries. The scats of grizzlies are generally a bit larger than those of the smaller black bears, which average about 1½ inches in diameter.

Other carnivores typically leave one or two relatively dry, thin logs rich in indigestible animal parts. Bones and fur are swallowed along with the meat, to reappear in the feces. The feces of wolves can be quite large—up to ¾ inch in diameter and

4 inches long. The scats of other carnivores are generally smaller, and are impossible to tell apart without accompanying tracks. Many of the smaller carnivores, likes weasels and martens, may have specific latrine sites within their territories. Each animal has scat that is scented with an individual musk, and the latrine sites are used to mark the boundaries of territories and keep out other animals of the same species.

Remains

Antlers that have been cast by caribou or moose are often found scattered about the landscape. These antlers are not the remains of kill sites, but are shed naturally by living animals each year. Because these antlers are cast in the depths of winter, they are a good indicator of winter range. In places where calcium and phosphorous are hard to come by, many animals chew these cast antlers to acquire the nutrients needed for bone

The scattered bones of this bull caribou indicate that he was likely a victim of predation.

growth. Rodents are particularly avid antler chewers, but moose and caribou will also gnaw on cast antlers to help satisfy their dietary requirements. As a result, cast antlers rarely last more than a couple of years on the open tundra. Dall sheep and other animals with true horns do not shed them, and horn casings for these animals indicate a kill site.

In many cases, you can tell a lot about how an animal died by examining the assemblage of bones remaining on the kill site. Never approach a fresh kill site, because its owner may be nearby and will usually defend its kill vigorously. The presence of ravens and magpies often indicates a fresh kill, and sites with a lingering odor of decay should be avoided. Bears in particular are dangerous near their kills. A fresh bear kill can often be identified by the fact that bears like to cover their kills with brush and debris in order to protect the meat from scavengers. The bear may tear up the ground within a 50-yard radius of the kill, in order to cover it, or may leave the kill completely exposed. Older kill sites, where the bleached bones are all that remain of the animal, are the only ones that can be approached safely.

Animals that die of natural causes will often be scavenged, making it difficult to determine the true cause of death. When wolves make a kill, the carcass is typically torn limb from limb and scattered around the site. The leg bones often have their ends chewed off as the wolves seek the fatty marrow inside. In addition, delicate bones, like the ones found in the nasal region of the skull, are often chewed off and ingested. Punctures in the thick cranium of an animal indicate a bear kill, as wolves rarely kill in this way. Smaller scavengers, like foxes and ravens, may scatter the bones a bit, but are unable to break the larger leg bones, and thus these long bones will be found whole. If the skeleton appears to be fairly complete intact, then the animal probably died of natural causes and was never scavenged by large animals.

You can also determine the physical condition of the animal when it died by evaluating the marrow, which is found in the long bones of the fore and hind limbs. This marrow often lasts almost indefinitely in the cold Alaskan soil, and can be evaluated years after the death of the animal. To find the marrow, crack open a leg bone at the center, exposing the hollow, marrow-filled cavity. An animal in good condition will have fatty marrow that has a yellow tint and a greasy consistency like butter. An animal that was starving when it died will have almost no fat in the marrow, which will be watery and dark red. On a kill site made by large predators, the marrow will often have been eaten already by the animals that made the kill.

9 Nature's Bounty

FAMILIARITY with a landscape entails a thorough knowledge of both the obstacles and the opportunities found there. One opportunity that the Alaskan wilderness offers knowledgeable travelers is a wide variety of edible wild food, which can be used to supplement meals or as emergency rations when store-bought food runs out. Edible plants and game are patchily distributed throughout the landscape, and by no means can they be counted on with absolute certainty. However, if you become familiar with some of the most important food sources available in the Alaskan wilderness, you can increase the quality of your trip by recognizing and taking advantage of them. Bear in mind, however, that other creatures may also be counting on these food sources to sustain themselves. Gather wild foods sparingly, and always make sure that plenty remains for the wild inhabitants that depend on it.

Berries

Throughout evolutionary time, plants have faced the problem of how to disperse their seeds so that they might colonize new habitats. Some plants used the wind for seed dispersal, and attached wings or parachutes to their seeds to speed their travels. Other plants, like the coconut, relied on water to transport their seeds. Some plants developed no special adaptations at all, and their seeds fell next to the parent plant, to compete with the larger adult. When the dinosaurs went extinct and mammals and birds diversified into a broad variety of forms, many higher plants developed fruits in order to coax these warm-blooded creatures into carrying their seeds from place to place. The plants, for their part, provided a nutritious, highly visible food package, with tough seeds within that could resist digestion. After the seeds passed through the digestive tract of their erstwhile host, they were deposited in a pile of dung rich in the nutrients that the young plant needed for rapid growth.

Humankind has been taking advantage of this palatable food source for millennia. The gathering of wild berries is an integral part of most surviving primitive cultures. Alaska is home to a variety of delicious edible fruits that grow in wild profusion throughout the state. Here are some of the most common and tasty varieties that you can pick as you make your way through the wilderness.

Blueberries. These are by far the most common and abundant berries in the state of Alaska. They range throughout the state, from the rain-drenched southeastern forests to the arid ridges of the Arctic coastal plain. There are four species of blueberry in Alaska, as well as the closely related red huckleberry. These plants take on a variety of growth forms, from tall, spindly shrubs in forested areas to the dwarf varieties found on open tundra. All have sweet, delicious fruits that are similar to commercial blueberries in taste. Alaskan blueberries range from pea-size up to the size of a thimble.

Blueberry

Look for blueberry plants on well-drained ridges in loose forests with a sparse understory. In tundra areas, blueberries often grow in association with light-colored ground lichens. Bog varieties can be found in wet, hummocky areas, while tall-bush types are most often found in open-canopy forests and clearcuts. The leaves of the blueberry plant are small, gray-green ovals sometimes marked by tiny serrations near their tips. The fruits ripen in mid-August, and are ready for picking when a white, waxy coating of pectin covers the deep blue fruit. These fruits are wonderful when eaten fresh, and also make excellent jams, jellies, and pies.

Lowbush Cranberries. Known in Sweden as lingonberries, these relatives of the blueberry form a dense, matlike ground cover. These evergreen shrubs rarely exceed 6 inches in height and have shiny, dark green oval leaves with smooth edges. The sour berries are a translucent deep red color and ripen in late August. They are sweetest after the first frost. These berries can be found in bogs, open spruce and birch forests, and tundra. The fruit is most commonly used for jams and jellies, and also makes excellent syrup and liqueur.

Red Currants. These low-growing shrubs inhabit most of south-central and interior Alaska. They may grow prostrate on the ground as a creeping vine, or attain heights of 2 to 3 feet when erect. The leaves are large and maple-shaped with toothed edges. The bark of mature plants has a shredded texture. The bright red, translucent berries grow in

Red Currants

clusters on special flowering stalks. Look for this shrub in spruce and birch forests, as well as in brush ravines above the treeline. The fruits are edible, and are similar in taste to commercial currants.

Crowberries. These tiny, mat-forming evergreens look almost like miniature spruces, due to their narrow, needlelike leaves. The matte black berry matures in mid-August, and can be collected in great numbers on rocky, well-drained slopes. The berries have a perfumy flavor, which is followed by a rather bitter aftertaste.

Crowberry

These berries often seem almost dry because of the large number of good-sized seeds contained within. They can be eaten raw, or mixed with other berries in jams and pies.

Bearberries. These tiny shrubs are often mistaken for herbaceous weeds, because the woody stalk is often invisible upon first glance. The leaves are narrow at the base, widening to an oval tip. They are generally found clustered around a single rooting point in a basal rosette, prostrate on the ground. You can find bearberries growing in patches on fairly moist soil in open forests and on tundra. The berries of the forest variety are translucent red, while the alpine variety sports jet black berries. You will have to lift up the leaves and look underneath for the berry clusters, which usually come in twos and threes. The berries mature in August and are edible, although they lack a strong taste.

Bearberry

Raspberries. This popular commercial fruit grows wild throughout central and southern Alaska. Look for the prickly vines in disturbed parts of the forest (clearcuts, roadsides, and small burns). The leaves are compound, with three pointed-oval leaflets that have toothed edges. The berries are a dusky red purple, and have hollow centers when picked. The seedy aggregate fruits have the same sweet-tart taste as their domestic relatives, and make excellent trailside snacks.

Cloudberries. These bog-dwelling plants grow in association with permafrost throughout interior and northern Alaska. They are often found in association with moss mats and black spruce, which share the cloudberry's frigid habitats. This low-growing plant can be recognized by its large, maple-shaped leaves

Cloudberry

with toothed edges. The outer part of the leaves is often rimmed with purple. This close relative of the raspberry has aggregate fruits that have hollow centers when picked. Pink to bright orange when ripe, and quite large (about the size of the end of your thumb), the brightly colored berries look like outlandish lightbulbs when met in their otherwise uniform green habitats. They are sweet with a strong, distinctive flavor like that of baked apples. The seeds are large and numerous. These fruits are tasty when eaten fresh, and make outstanding pies.

Salmonberries. Another member of the raspberry family, the salmonberry inhabits moist, open slopes in coastal areas of southern and southeastern Alaska. The berries are orange to dark red when ripe, mild tasting, and full of seeds. Look for dense thickets of these plants in recent clearcuts. The berries make good eating along the trail, but are a bit seedy for cooking purposes.

Salmonberry

Rose Hips. The wild rose produces edible fruits called hips in late summer. Wild roses are common in spruce and birch forest and in disturbed sites within the forest. These small shrubs are characterized by prickly stems and compound leaves with five oval, toothed leaflets. The fruits are not technically berries, but resemble more closely the pulpy flesh of apples. They have a mealy texture and a slightly sweet taste, and are rich in vitamin C. Rose hips can be eaten raw, or can be made into syrup or a mealy spread similar to apple butter.

Rose Hips

Baneberries. This plant has the only poisonous berries to be found in most of Alaska, and should be avoided at all costs.

The leaves are compound and complex, with a fernlike arrangement of toothed oval leaflets. The berries are waxy white or red, and grow in clusters on erect stalks that rise from top of the plant. The toxin contained in these berries is highly potent, and can be fatal if ingested.

Baneberry

Other Plants

There are a number of other plants that are useful to back-packers as food sources and for other purposes. These plants are not as immediately obvious as brightly colored berries and may be more difficult to find. Labrador tea, a small, woody plant that grows on well-drained soils throughout the boreal North, has leaves that can be boiled to make a flavorful drink. This plant can be recognized by its narrow, leathery leaves that grow alternately from the main stalk. The leaves are dark green and shiny on top, with a pale, woolly underside. The young leaves of willow shrubs have few defensive tannins, and can be consumed as a sort of salad. The soft inner bark of quaking aspen was used by Native Americans to make a sort of flour from which bread was baked.

Mushrooms

Several species of edible mushrooms are common in Alaska and the Yukon. However, identifying them can be a tricky proposition: Deadly varieties often look quite similar to their edible cousins. To identify edible mushrooms, you must examine the characteristics of the stem, cap, and gills. In some cases chemical tests may be required. The identification of edible wild mushrooms would take an entire text in itself, and so this information cannot be presented here. Consult a mycologist or other local expert before you eat wild mushrooms, no matter how innocuous they look.

Invertebrates as Emergency Food

Insects and other invertebrates are looked upon with distaste by most gourmands in Western cultures. However, grubs and beetles are an important part of the diet in many developing countries. Indeed, grasshoppers and ants are delicacies in many parts of the world, and there is no doubt that insects are a fine source of protein. If you find yourself short of food in a wilderness setting, your best strategy is to set aside your cultural tastes and look to invertebrates as a potential food source.

The richest source of insect food in Arctic environments is found in lakes and streams. The larval forms of some winged insects can be found in aquatic environments in densities that make them profitable to collect. By turning over logs and stones, you can find a wealth of caddis and stonefly nymphs. The outlet streams of lakes are especially productive places to hunt for aquatic insects, as are pools in clear-flowing streams. When ice covers the surface of a lake, you can assure yourself of an abundant food supply simply by cutting a hole through the ice. Freshwater shrimp and tiny blackfish will be attracted to the light, and you can scoop them out of the water with a cup.

On land, look for rotting vegetation to find insects and other arthropods. Rotting stumps and logs are especially good places to look. Where deciduous trees are abundant, look below the layer of leaf litter at the soil's surface to find burrowing insects and grubs. (Conifer needles make poor food for insects, so the duff below spruce trees is relatively barren of insect life.) Invertebrates can be fried to make them more palatable, but even then they're not exactly a gourmet's delight.

Fish

Alaska's streams and lakes provide some of the finest fishing to be found anywhere on earth. The abundance of fish can be great in clear streams and lakes that sustain a high level of algae growth, while sport fish may be almost entirely absent in streams or rivers that carry heavy loads of glacial silt. Many areas near roads and towns have been overfished by Alaska's summer visitors, but the watersheds in the backcountry are still relatively untouched. Thus, backpackers avail themselves of Alaska's best fishing opportunities, a prospect that makes bringing rod and reel along a profitable proposition. Most of Alaska's game fish are quite tasty when properly prepared, and can serve as a delicious supplement to camping fare, as well as a primary food supply for travelers who find themselves in emergency circumstances.

In the far northern waters of Alaska, growing seasons are short, and freshwater fish take a long time to reach eating size. Steady fishing pressure, even when it is relatively light, can decimate fish populations in a short period of time. In the interest of maintaining healthy fish populations, you should release all fish that you do not intend to eat. In this manner, you can ensure that future anglers have access to the same opportunities that you enjoyed. Check with local authorities to find out what licenses are required for sport fishing, and what the local catch limits are.

Alaska's freshwater systems contain two basic types of fish: freshwater fish and anadromous fish. Freshwater fish spend their entire life cycle in fresh water, and tend to grow at a slow rate. Anadromous fish abandon freshwater environments in a run to the sea when they approach adulthood. At sea, they have access to a much richer food base, which allows them to grow rapidly and achieve great size. These anadromous fish undertake long migrations to spawn in the same streams where they were born, and these spawning runs provide wonderful fishing opportunities for anglers. Some anadromous fishes, such as steelhead and Dolly Varden trout, can return to fresh water repeatedly to spawn. Pacific salmon, on the other hand, use up their entire body reserves in one spawning effort, and die immediately thereafter.

Trout and Char. These popular game fish occur throughout Alaska, and include both freshwater and anadromous varieties. The freshwater rainbow and its seagoing cousin, the steelhead, inhabit clear streams and lakes from south-central Alaska through the Copper River Basin and into southeast Alaska. These fish are prized for their fighting ability, and frequently jump clear of the water when hooked. Arctic char dominate interior Alaska and the North Slope. Their oily, orange-colored flesh provides a tasty treat for backpackers in remote areas. Dolly Varden trout are seagoing fish that abound in south-central and southeast Alaska, and are generally quite unwary. Lake trout have been planted in a number of lakes in interior Alaska, and are one of the most sought-after game fish in the Yukon Territories. Native cutthroat trout still inhabit many of the clear-flowing streams in southeast Alaska.

The diet of these fish is made up almost entirely of aquatic insects, both the subsurface larval forms and the flying adults that return to the water to lay their eggs. Caddisflies, stoneflies, and mayflies make up the bulk of the diet. Larger, older trout will also hunt for small fish if they are available. Small spoons and spinners, as well as a wide variety of flies, make the best lures for catching these wily game fish.

Arctic Grayling. These unusual fish are distant relatives of trout and are characterized by a large, sail-like dorsal fin. In spawning colors, grayling are an iridescent gray, with bright spots on their dorsal fins that range from pink to deep purple. They are common in streams and lakes in interior and northern Alaska, and are readily fooled by lures and flies. An average adult grayling weighs about a pound, making a perfect pan-sized meal. The flesh is similar to that of trout, but has a slightly smoky flavor.

Pike. These long, slender inhabitants of weedy shallows are fairly common in lakes and slow-moving river sloughs in interior Alaska. They are ambush predators, and make their living by lying in wait in weed beds for unwary prey to pass by. Pike are easiest to catch with large spoons and casting plugs, but will also take large streamers. These fish have incredibly sharp teeth that can easily snap monofilament, and thus many pike anglers

Grayling are the most common game fish in the interior.

prefer to attach a wire leader ahead of their lure. Pike average about 15 pounds in weight, but can reach 40 pounds. Their flesh is flaky and white, but has lots of bones that make it a challenge to eat.

Salmon. The Pacific salmon native to Alaska are all anadromous and return to their spawning streams at varying times of the year. Each run is fairly predictable in its timing. Check with local sporting goods stores to find out when the salmon are running locally. (Also see "The Explorer's Directory" at the back of this book.) Size and creel limits vary widely from drainage to drainage, so it will be necessary to consult the tome-like state fishing regulations to make sure that your catch can legally be kept. Salmon can also be caught offshore if you have access to a seaworthy boat. Charter services are available statewide in coastal areas.

Salmon are in a race with time from the moment they enter fresh water. Their digestive and immune systems are broken down and used for energy to fuel their spawning drives. Without an effective immune system, bacteria and fungi attack the fish and with time they begin to decompose while still living.

Indeed, salmon harbor toxic bacteria in the slime around their mouths that can cause "salmon sickness" in humans if they come in contact with an open cut. As a result of their progressive rotting "on the hoof," silvery fish fresh from the sea are much better eating than the older, "spawned-out" hulks that occur later in the run. Because these fish reabsorb their digestive organs once they enter fresh water, they do not eat at all, and anglers must attempt to anger the spawning fish using brightly colored, flashy lures and flies. Salmon will also crush the eggs of other fish that they encounter on their migration, so cured salmon eggs are also a popular bait.

There are five species of salmon in Alaska. The largest is the king salmon or chinook, which may attain weights in excess of 80 pounds. More typically, kings occur in the 30- to 40-pound range, and have a light pink flesh that is firm and tasty. Silver or coho salmon range from 10 to 20 pounds, and have deep pink flesh that is prized by gourmands the world over. The salmon of choice for most Alaskans are the red, or sockeye, salmon, which are quite common and range from 5 to 15 pounds. Pink salmon are also known as humpies for the prominent shoulder hump of spawning males, and have pink flesh of only moderate quality. Chum salmon rate at the bottom of the totem pole, and have a mealy flesh that is best suited to feeding sled dogs.

Other Fish. The inconnu, or sheefish, is a piscivorous (fish-eating) whitefish found in the major rivers of the interior north of Fairbanks. An excellent sport fish, the inconnu reaches a considerable size; 15-pound specimens are not uncommon. The relative obscurity of this fish is reflected in its name, which translates as "unknown" in French. The Arctic cisco is an anadromous whitefish of the North Slope. Adults attain average weights of between 2 and 3 pounds, and make good (although bony) eating. Many other species of whitefish inhabit freshwater systems throughout the state. They eat aquatic invertebrates for the most part, and have tiny mouths. Whitefish are especially tasty when smoked. The burbot, a freshwater member of the codfish family, resides in deep water in lakes and larger rivers throughout Alaska. It is an excellent food fish, with flaky, white flesh that is almost totally devoid of bones.

Stream-Fishing Strategy

As in crossing streams, the most important lesson in fishing Alaskan streams is learning to read the water. Fish like to hang out in eddies and pools where current flow is slight. At the same time, drifting food is most abundant in faster-running riffle areas. Thus the best spots to look for feeding fish are places where fish lying in eddies have easy access to nearby fast-flowing sections, which bring in food. In general, the best positions are occupied by the largest fish, while small fish must make do with lesser positions.

When fishing in stream systems, look for obstructions that block current in a fast-flowing stretch. Submerged boulders, logs, and even beaver dams provide fish with hiding cover and shelter from the current. Undercut banks on the outside of curves, as well as overhanging willow and alder, also provide admirable cover for stream fish. Pocket water, which is typified by numerous small pools separated by brief cascades, provides some of the most entertaining and productive fishing around. Larger pools also harbor large fish, although these fish may move up into faster water to feed. Fast, smooth runs and un-broken riffles make poor fish habitats.

How to Fish Lakes

Lakes are more difficult to evaluate from the standpoint of find-ing fish. Most species of lake-dwelling fish move about in large schools. This phenomenon results in boom-or-bust fishing; if you can find the fish, you are in for a real bonanza. Lakes are not completely uniform habitats, and some areas consistently pro-duce more fish than others. Around the periphery of lakes, many fish cruise the edges of shelves or dropoffs where they can quickly retreat into deeper water when disturbed. Sub-merged humps and islands also attract schools of fish. The deltas where inlet streams enter a lake are also good places to look, because they carry particles of food into the lake in a continuous flow. Many lake fish also use inlet and outlet streams for spawning, and thus these areas are also good places to look for fish. In general, anglers can fish smaller lakes from the shoreline, while they may need a boat to fish large lakes effectively.

Equipment

Advances in fishing tackle have resulted in specialized fishing equipment just for backpackers. New compact and portable rods featuring nested, telescoped, and break-apart designs are now available. Fishing reels are also becoming smaller and lighter. The most advanced pack rods are priced out of reach of most backpackers, but good compromise packages can be put together on a fairly small budget. For versatility, the best combination is a portable fly rod coupled with fly reel and tackle or attached to a small spinning reel to cast spinners, spoons, and plugs. Steer clear of heavy, bulky equipment that will overmatch your quarry and put more weight on your back than necessary.

A tiny tackle box that holds a variety of spinners, spoons, and flies will fit neatly into one of the side pockets of your pack. Think small and light; the fish in Alaska's backcountry are not particularly finicky, and will take almost anything if it is presented to them properly. If fishing is to be a primary focus of your expedition, you might think about bringing a small landing net and some hip boots as well. Small, inflatable doughnut floats are available for the true fanatic who wants to pack the capabilities of a boat into the backcountry.

Tickling for Trout

You can catch trout and grayling even if you do not have a rod and reel, through a time-honored method known as tickling. In order to accomplish this feat, you must first chase the fish under a rock or undercut bank. The fish will lie still, allowing you to slowly slip your hands under it. The warmth of your hands on the belly of the fish will lull it into a relaxed state. Now, cupping the fish in your hands, slowly ease it out of the water, and then throw it onto the bank. This technique works well in small streams, but is almost impossible to execute successfully in larger ones.

Afterword

ALASKA can become an addiction; it gets into your blood and draws you back again and again. My first experience with the state came during my college years, in the form of a summer of backpacking throughout the North Country. Despite traveling throughout the Rocky Mountain West, I had never set eyes on a vast expanse of country that had not been fenced off, clearcut, or subdivided. When I crossed the 60th parallel, I entered a world that had never submitted to the machinations of modern human society, that still retained all of the wild character, all of the inherent perils of the wilderness that it possessed when the first explorers wandered into the land over 10,000 years ago. Here was a place where I could test my skills against the rigors of the Arctic, where I could become acquainted with my innermost drives, and where I could fully come to appreciate my own small stature in the context of a vast and ancient land.

I set about exploring all of the wilderness corners of the Far North that I could reach with my borrowed-and-beaten vehicle. One of my first forays into the backcountry took me into the southern fringes of the Wrangell Mountains. I was told that there were no trails here, that I would have to follow moose trails, sheep tracks, and my own native sense to reach my destination of Dixie Pass. It was overcast as I left, but following my own motto of "go anyway," I started thrashing my way through the willow. The route followed the valley of a small stream, swollen by recent rains until it gushed across its boulder-strewn course. The brush thinned as I gained altitude, but the valley walls constricted around the muddy torrent, and I was forced to make numerous fords.

The head of the valley was surrounded by steep, tundra-clad slopes. There was no obvious route to the pass, so I resorted to scrambling up across the slippery meadows. Monkshood and forget-me-not were scattered over the turf, providing a pleasant diversion from the grueling climb. Soon, sheep trails offered easier footing, and I followed them into a low saddle. A tinkle of loose shale announced the presence of a dozen Dall sheep on the slopes above; they paced nervously about, unsure of whether or not to flee from such an ungainly creature. Before long, they settled down to feeding once more. Finally reaching Dixie Pass, I pitched my tiny bivouac tent and cooked my dinner as the curious rams watched from the slopes above.

The clouds rolled in during the night, and soon a heavy rain started to fall. In the gray hours around midnight, the noise stopped, and I was awakened by an increasing weight on my hips. Opening the tent flap, I discovered a deep accumulation of snow had weighed down my tent, and I spent the balance of the night in a running battle to keep the sagging structure erect. The clouds had broken into tattered scarves by morning, and tendrils of mist moved along the ragged summits that encircled my camp. Snow blanketed the peaks to a depth of half a foot, and I packed up my gear with a certain amount of trepidation in light of the slippery descent that lay ahead.

Glissading down from the pass turned out to be the easy part of the trek. The brush on the valley floor was soaked by the new rain, which also showed a striking affinity for my rather inadequate clothes. Near the trailhead I discovered a camp scattered across the trail—sleeping bags, clothing, and gear strewn everywhere. I began to call out to any bear that might be near, and poked around a bit before deciding that no one was around. At the trailhead, I met the cause of the mess: A young couple had hiked in with only a tarp for shelter, and as the pouring rain soaked through their sleeping bags, they were forced to make a hasty midnight retreat to the warmth of their vehicle.

Brooding clouds over Mush Lake in the Yukon's Kluane National Park

The summer progressed in such a fashion, with mad dashes between trailheads and long, languorous forays into the backcountry. It gave me a first glimpse into a country that would require several lifetimes to explore fully. When I returned to Montana, my hunger for wilderness was satisfied, and my curiosity about Alaska and other points north was slaked. Or so I thought.

It is said that once you have visited Alaska, you are certain to return. My own predilection for the prairies and forests of Montana bound me close to home, but my career track soon turned my eyes northward again. Alaska is one of the last places on the continent where a biologist can study a pristine ecosystem, and as I looked for an attractive place to do field research for a master's degree in wildlife management, Alaska was the obvious choice. I was fortunate enough to draw a study on moose behavior in the Alaska Range, where I could work with animals that had no fear of humans; I could mingle freely in breeding groups during the heart of the rut, without exciting attention from my subjects. It was relaxing to share the company of animals that have such a peaceful and deliberate lifestyle, and through two seasons I came to appreciate the complexity and majesty of this largest of American deer.

But the cold months of the year were long and dark, and I fought a losing battle with my pineal gland to remain active and alert during the depths of the interior winters. With degree in hand, I headed south to seek my fortune, forsaking biology for writing (where the job prospects are better). But it was only 2 years before I found myself bounding across the Arctic tundra once more, for a season in the sun that never sets. I suppose that I will always be coming back, and that my curiosity will never be satisfied. I am sure that I will never see all that is magnificent even if I spend a lifetime of poking around in this northwestern corner of the continent.

I am fortunate to live at this time, when people still have a few untracked refuges from their own insanity. The Arctic lands possess a magnificence that rip the words from your mind and leave you staring into the distance, mouth hanging open, senses overloaded in the vain effort to absorb the immensity of the country and hold it inside your mind forever. This land is huge, and we are small; we do not travel over the land but merge into its vastness, becoming active players on a wild and ancient stage.

But even this indomitable country is shrinking, as we intelligent ants nibble away at its fringes. Some Alaskans look into the untracked distance and think that it is limitless, that it will always remain wild. Others look south to the "outside" world, with its strip malls and wheat fields, suburbs and feedlots, and know with a knowledge born of painful experience that their heritage of wild places in this northern sweep of the globe cannot be maintained without vigilance and forethought. We who have inherited 48 states that have been stripped bare, plowed under, fenced off, and cut into tiny sections; we who have seen the consequences of consumption without responsibility; we who have the science and technology to build an economy without destroying the ecosystem that made it possible, still have Alaska and northwestern Canada.

Our predecessors had scant knowledge of the consequences of unlimited development; ecology had not yet been invented. We now have this knowledge, and with it the chance and the responsibility to pass on to our grandchildren the opportunities to experience nature in its purest form. In Alaska, we have the ability to build a thriving economy that integrates itself into the natural rhythms of Alaska's ecosystems without destroying them. In so doing we can maintain a high quality of life for our descendants to enjoy. Though the course of my own life may carry me elsewhere, I will return always to the land of the midnight sun, to remind myself of my place in the cosmos and my duty to preserve its balance. It is my hope that there are still wild and lonely places long after the borrowed atoms that make up my body have returned to the earth.

The Explorer's Directory

General Information

Alaska Department of Parks and Outdoor Recreation, 3700 Airport Way, Fairbanks, AK 99709-4613; 907-451-2695.

Alaska Division of Tourism, PO Box 110801, Juneau, AK 99811-0801; 907-465-2010.

Alaska Public Lands Information Center, 605 W. 4th Ave., Suite 105, Anchorage, AK 99501; 907-271-2737; TDD 907-271-2738.

Alaska Public Lands Information Center, 250 Cushman St., Suite 1A, Fairbanks, AK 99701; 907-456-0527; TDD 907-456-0532.

Alaska Public Lands Information Center, 50 Main St., Ketchikan, AK 99901; 907-228-6214; TDD 907-228-6237.

Alaska Public Lands Information Center, PO Box 359, Tok, AK 99780; 907-883-5667.

Bureau of Land Management, 1150 University Ave., Fairbanks, AK 99701; 907-474-2200.

US Fish and Wildlife Service, 1101 Tudor Rd., Anchorage, AK 99503; 907-786-3486.

Specific Area Information

Arctic National Wildlife Refuge, 101 12th Ave., Fairbanks, AK 99701; 907-456-0250.

Chugach National Forest, 3301 C St., Suite 300, Anchorage, AK 99503-3998.

Denali National Park and Preserve, PO Box 9, Denali Park, AK 99755; 907-683-2294; bus and campground reservations 800-622-7275.

Gates of the Arctic National Park and Preserve, Box 74680, Fairbanks, AK 99707-4680; 907-456-0281.

Katmai National Park, PO Box 7, King Salmon, AK 99613-0007; 907-246-3305.

Kenai Fjords National Park, PO Box 1727, Seward, AK 99664-1727; 907-224-3175.

Klondike Gold Rush National Historical Park, PO Box 517, Skagway, AK 99840-0517; 907-983-2921; Canadian Chilkoot Trail information 403-668-2116.

Lake Clark National Park, 4230 University Dr., Suite 311, Anchorage, AK 99508; 907-271-3751.

Tongass National Forest, 101 Egan Dr., Juneau, AK 99801; 907-586-8751; TDD 907-586-7814; cabin reservations 907-228-6219.

Wrangell–St. Elias National Park and Preserve, PO Box 29, Glenallen, AK 99588-0029; 907-822-5234

Yukon-Charley National Preserve, PO Box 167, Eagle, AK 99738; 907-547-2233

Native Corporations

Ahtna, Inc. (Copper River Basin), 2701 Fairbanks St., Anchorage, AK 99503.

Aleut Corp. (Aleutian Islands), 1 Aleut Plaza, 4000 Old Seward Hwy., Suite 300, Anchorage, AK 99503.

Arctic Slope Regional Corp. (North Slope), 313 E St., Suite 5, Anchorage, AK 99501.

Bering Straits Native Corp. (Seward Peninsula), PO Box 100220, Anchorage, AK 99510.

Calista Corp. (Yukon-Kuskokwim Delta), 516 Denali St., Anchorage, AK 99510.

Chugach Alaska Corp. (South-central Coast), 3000 A St., Suite 400, Anchorage, AK 99503.

Cook Inlet Region, Inc., 2525 C St., Anchorage, AK 99503.

Doyon, Ltd. (Interior Alaska), 201 First Ave., Suite 200, Fairbanks, AK 99701.

Koniag, Inc. (Kodiak Island), PO Box 786, Kodiak, AK 99615.

NANA Corp. (Lower Kobuk Valley), 4706 Harding Dr., Anchorage, AK 99503.

Sealaska Corp. (Southeast Alaska), One Sealaska Plaza, Juneau, AK 99801.

Yukon Territories

Kluane National Park Reserve, Box 5495, Haines Junction, YT Y0B 1L0 Canada; 403-634-2251.

Tourism Yukon, PO Box 2703, Whitehorse, YT Y1A 2C6 Canada; 403-667-5340.

Sources of Topographic Maps

US Geological Survey, 4230 University Dr., Rm. 101, Anchorage, AK 99508; 907-786-7011.

EFIC Map Office/Geodata Center, Geophysical Institute, University of Alaska, 903 Koyukuk Dr., Fairbanks, AK 99775-7320; 907-474-6960.

Exploration and Geological Services Division, 200 Main St., #345, Whitehorse, Yukon Y1A 2B5 Canada.

Transportation Information

Alaska Marine Highway System, PO Box 25535, Juneau, AK 99801-5535; 800-642-0066.
Alaska Railroad, 411 W. First Ave., Anchorage, AK 99501; 800-544-0552.

Salmon Spawning Runs

Watershed	Salmon Species	Freshwater Run
Yukon & Kuskokwim Rivers	Chinook (King)	June–Aug
	Coho (Silver)	Sept–Nov
	Chum (Dog)	mid-June–Dec
Tanana River	Chinook (King)	July
	Coho (Silver)	mid-Sept–mid-Nov
	Chum (Dog)	July–Aug, Oct–Nov
Susitna River	Chinook (King)	mid-May–early Aug
	Sockeye (Red)	June–mid-Sept
	Coho (Silver)	mid-July–early Oct
	Pink (Humpy)	mid-July–early Aug
	Chum (Dog)	mid-July–Sept
Matanuska River	Chinook (King)	mid-May–early Aug
& Anchorage Area	Sockeye (Red)	mid-June–mid-Aug
	Coho (Silver)	mid-July–early Oct
	Pink (Humpy)	mid-June–mid-Aug
	Chum (Dog)	mid-July–Sept
Kenai Peninsula	Chinook (King)	mid-May–July
	Sockeye (Red)	mid-May–mid-Aug
	Coho (Silver)	mid-July–Jan
	Pink (Humpy)	mid-July–mid-Sept
Copper River &	Chinook (King)	mid-June–mid-July
Prince William Sound	Sockeye (Red)	July–Aug
	Coho (Silver)	mid-Aug–early Sept
Southeast Alaska	Chinook (King)	mid-May–Aug
(North of Cape Fanshaw)	Sockeye (Red)	June–Sept
	Coho (Silver)	Sept–Nov
	Pink (Humpy)	July–Sept
	Chum (Dog)	June–Oct
Southeast Alaska	Chinook (King)	mid-May–mid-Aug
(South of Cape Fanshaw)	Sockeye (Red)	June–Aug
	Coho (Silver)	mid-June–early Nov
	Pink (Humpy)	July–Oct
	Chum (Dog)	July–late Oct

For Further Reading

GENERAL INFORMATION ON ALASKA

The Alaska Almanac. Anchorage: Alaska Northwest Books, published annually.

Alaska Atlas and Gazetteer. Freeport, Maine: DeLorme Mapping, 1992.

Kresge, David T., Thomas A. Morehouse, and George W. Rogers. *Issues in Alaska Development.* Seattle: University of Washington Press, 1977.

Schorr, Alan E. *Alaska Place Names.* Juneau: Denali Press, 1991.

TRAVEL GUIDES

The Alaska Wilderness Milepost. Edmonds, Washington: Alaska Northwest Books, 1986.

Gage, S.R. *A Walk on the Canol Road.* New York: Mosaic Press, 1990.

Lanz, Walter. *Along the Dempster.* Vancouver: Oak House Publishing, 1985.

The Milepost. Anchorage: Alaska Research Company, published annually.

Miller, Mike, and Marilyn Miller. *Camping Alaska and Canada's Yukon: The Motorist's Handbook to North Country Campgrounds and Roadways.* Seattle: Pacific Search Press, 1987.

Merry, Wayne. *Official Wilderness First Aid Guide.* Ontario: Firefly Books, 1994.

Molvar, Erik. *Alaska-Yukon Scenic Drives.* Helena, Montana: Falcon Press, 1996.

Nierenburg, Jon. *A Backcountry Companion to Denali National Park.* Anchorage: Alaska Natural History Association, 1990.

Simmerman, Nancy L. *Alaska Parklands: A Complete Guide.* Seattle: Mountaineers Books, 1983.

———. *55 Ways to the Wilderness.* Seattle: Mountaineers Books, 1985.

NATURAL HISTORY

Alaska Wild Berry Guide and Cookbook. Seattle: Alaska Northwest Books, 1989.

Armstrong, Robert H. *Guide to the Birds of Alaska.* Edmonds, Washington: Alaska Northwest Books, 1990.

Guthrie, R.D. *Frozen Fauna of the Mammoth Steppe.* Chicago: University of Chicago Press, 1990.

Murie, Adolph. *The Grizzlies of Mt. McKinley.* National Park Service Scientific Monograph Series no. 14. Washington, DC: US Goverment Printing Office, 1981.

———. *The Wolves of Mt. McKinley.* Seattle: University of Washington Press, 1985.

Viereck, Leslie A., and Elbert L. Little Jr. *Alaska Trees and Shrubs.* Fairbanks: University of Alaska Press, 1986.

TRUE ADVENTURE/HISTORY

Allen, Lt. Henry. *An Expedition to the Copper, Tanana, and Koyukuk Rivers in 1885.* Seattle: Alaska Northwest Books.

Glenn, Edwin F. "Report of Captain Edwin F. Glenn on Explorations in Alaska." In *Reports of Explorations in the Territory of Alaska.* Washington, DC: US Government Printing Office, 1899.

Goetzman, William H., and Kay Sloan. *Looking Far North: The Harriman Expedition to Alaska, 1899.* Princeton: Princeton University Press, 1982.

Herron, John H. *Explorations in Alaska, 1899, for an All-American Overland Route from Cook Inlet, Pacific Ocean, to the Yukon.* Washington, DC: US Government Printing Office, 1909.

Lopez, Barry. *Arctic Dreams.* New York: Scribner, 1986.

Marshall, Robert. *Alaska Wilderness: Exploring the Central Brooks Range.* Second ed. Berkeley: University of California Press, 1970.

———. *Arctic Village.* Fairbanks: University of Alaska Press, 1991.

Miller, Debbie S. *Midnight Wilderness: Journeys in Alaska's Arctic National Wildlife Refuge.* San Francisco: Sierra Club Books, 1990.

Muir, John. *Travels in Alaska.* Boston: Houghton Mifflin, 1979.

Murie, Adolph. *A Naturalist in Alaska.* Tucson: University of Arizona Press, 1990.

Murie, Margaret. *Two in the Far North.* Seattle: Alaska Northwest Publishing, 1978.

Nelson, Richard K. *Make Prayers to the Raven: A Koyukon View of the Northern Forest.* Chicago: University of Chicago Press, 1983.

———. *The Island Within.* San Francisco: North Point Press, 1989.

Powell, Addison M. *Trailing and Camping in Alaska.* New York: Wessels and Bissell, 1900.

Stuck, Hudson. *The Ascent of Denali.* Lincoln: University of Nebraska Press, 1989.

Index

strategies, 97-101
See also Expeditions
History of Alaska, 12-15, 34
Hitchhiking, 36-37
Hunting, 30-31, 35
Hypothermia, 142-144

Ice axes, 127, 129-132, 137
Insects, 25, 147, 171-172, 199
Inside Passage, 28, 37, 38, 47-48
Interior lowlands, 22, 39, 108, 182
Intertidal zone, 46, 141-142
Ivvavik National Park, 51

Kachemak Bay State Park, 46
Kahiltna Glacier, 134
Katmai National Park, 48
Kenai Fjords National Park, 45-46, 180
Kenai National Wildlife Refuge, 44, 178
Kenai Peninsula, 45, 46, 109, 182
Kennecott copper mine, 44
Klondike, 47
Kluane National Park, 44, 49, 179
Kodiak Island, 37

Lagomorphs, 183
Land ownership, 33-35
Latrine sites, 159-161
Layering, 53-56, 143
Lost, what to do when, 94-95

Mackenzie Mountains, 51
Maps. *See* Topographic maps
Map skills. *See* Compass skills
Marine mammals, 47
Marshall, Bob, 112
Midnight sun, 26-27
Moose, 31, 169-170, 177-178
Mountaineering, 15-16, 57, 127, 134, 135, 138-140
Mountain goats, 180
Mount McKinley. *See* Denali National Park
Muir, John, 27
Muskox, 176-177

Nahanni National Park, 51
National Park Service, 35, 40, 47
Navigation
  celestial, 92-93
  by compass, 86-87
  establishing baseline, 88
  pitfalls, 91
  straight-line course, 89-91
  triangulation, 88-89
  See also Topographic maps
Northern lights, 27-28
North Magnetic Pole, 85-86
North Slope, 22-23, 39
Northwest Territories, 48, 50-51
  wildlands, 35-36

Ogilvie Mountains, 50, 113, 176
Overflow ice, 123-124

Parks Highway, 41, 42, 43
Permafrost, 14, 36, 39, 50, 107-109
Permits, 29, 42, 47
Pests, 170-172
Petersville Road, 43
Pike, 201-202
Pleistocene Epoch, 12-13
Powell, Addison, 38, 171

Regions, 38-39
Resurrection Trail, 45
Richardson Mountains, 50, 113
Ridgelines, travel on, 102
Rivers, crossing. *See* Streams, crossing
Rock climbing, 41, 138-140
Rocky inclines, crossing, 124-126
Rodents, 170, 183
Roosevelt, President Franklin D., 178
Route, selection of
  cross-country hiking, 97-99
  game trails, 99-101
  ridgelines, 102
  streambeds, 102-104

Salmon, 31, 202-203
Seasons, 22-25
Sedge meadows, 113
Self-arrest, 129-132

About the Author

ERIK MOLVAR is a dedicated outdoorsman who has made a career of studying and exploring America's vast wilderness legacy. He has backpacked throughout the western half of the continent, and has written trail guides to Glacier National Park, Olympic National Park, the Bob Marshall Wilderness, and southern Arizona. Erik has made backcountry excursions throughout the 49th state, and has participated in several search-and-rescue efforts along the way. His master's studies at the University of Alaska have led to groundbreaking research in the ecology and behavior of moose in Denali National Park. It is the author's hope that his writings will bring greater awareness of and appreciation for our fast-shrinking wildlands.

Books from The Countryman Press
and Backcountry Publications

The Countryman Press and Backcountry Publications, long known for fine books on travel and outdoor recreation, offer a range of practical and readable manuals.

Outdoor How-To and General Interest

Backwoods Ethics: Environmental Issues for Hikers and Campers, by Laura and Guy Waterman
>Ways to protect the physical environment of our mountains and backcountry

Wilderness Ethics: Preserving the Spirit of Wildness, by Laura and Guy Waterman
>Evaluating the impact that even "environmentally conscious" values have on the wilderness experience

Camp and Trail Cooking Techniques: A Treasury of Skills and Recipes for All Outdoor Chefs, by Jim Capossela
>Loaded with how-to information and recipes for backpackers and for car campers

The Maze: A Desert Journey, by Lucy Rees
>A journey on horseback through the Arizona desert in search of an ancient stone carving

Fly-Fishing with Children: A Guide for Parents, by Philip Brunquell, M.D.
>"Philip Brunquell has captured the essence of parenting—the sharing of time, skills, passion, and values." *(The Washington Post)*

50 *Hikes* series

>Regional collections of hikes for hikers of all abilities; detailed directions, access information, and discussion of points of interest along the way. From Maine to lower Michigan.

We offer many more books on hiking, walking, fishing, and canoeing, plus books on travel, nature, and many other subjects.

Our books are available at bookstores, or they may be ordered directly from the publisher. For ordering information or for a complete catalog, please contact:

The Countryman Press
c/o W.W. Norton & Company, Inc.
800 Keystone Industrial Park
Scranton, PA 18512
http://web.wwnorton.com